The Illustrated History of
NOTTINGHAM'S SUBURBS

The Illustrated History of
NOTTINGHAM'S SUBURBS

GEOFFREY OLDFIELD

breedon **books**
PUBLISHING

First published in Great Britain in 2003 by
The Breedon Books Publishing Company Limited
Breedon House, 3 The Parker Centre,
Derby, DE21 4SZ.

ISBN 1 85983 351 9

Printed and bound by Butler & Tanner,
Frome, Somerset, England.

Cover printing by Lawrence-Allen Colour Printers,
Weston-super-Mare, Somerset, England.

CONTENTS

ACKNOWLEDGEMENTS

Illustrations which are marked LSL are reproduced by permission of Nottingham City Council Leisure and Community Services Local Studies Library. My thanks are due to the assistance given me by members of the staff of the Local Studies Library in producing the original illustrations and for the help and information they have given me, as they always do to everyone using the library.

Most of the other illustrations, apart from those of non-copyright sources, are the copyright of the author.

I also wish to thank Mrs Irene Young for efficiently typing the manuscript in spite of my handwriting.

INTRODUCTION

The *Landranger Ordnance Survey* maps depict in brown the urban or mainly built-up areas. That for Nottingham and Loughborough has such an area, almost a square of 10 miles each way. At its heart and covering about half the 100 square miles is the City of Nottingham. It is surrounded on all sides by what were, until 1974, mainly urban districts. They can be regarded as suburbs of Nottingham, primarily from their geographical situation. They do however have a wider justification for that description – economic, commercial, educational, cultural and transport links.

Nottingham itself, today a city of 18,000 acres, was until 1877 a borough of just under 2,000 acres. Moreover, until 1840 the built-up area was limited to about 150 acres. Because of ancient rights of the burgesses building could not take place on the remaining acres until legislation permitted. This was obtained and up to 1877 the former open fields became in effect the first Nottingham suburbs. Nottingham continued to grow in population and industrially. Surrounding the borough were a number of former villages which, like Nottingham, had grown in population, mainly because of common trading interests which took advantage of Nottingham's inability to expand on the common lands.

In 1877 the borough obtained a boundary extension Act which brought these villages within an extended town of some 10,000 acres, creating a second wave of new suburbs. The 20th century saw Nottingham's City Council trying to expand its boundaries once more in an effort to become a city on the scale of Birmingham or Manchester. The city was only partially successful, as central government permitted boundary extensions for the city only to the extent required for its policy of building council houses. This third wave of suburbs, on former agricultural land, brought the city's size to its present 18,000 acres.

The urban districts and some smaller parts of rural districts thus escaped becoming administratively part of the city and in 1974, under local government re-organisation, they were absorbed by four new district councils. This did not affect the reality of their affinity to the city as suburbs.

In writing this book, therefore, I have dealt with the development of the last 150 years in two parts, the first the growth of the city itself and the second its neighbours. For my sources I have been able to refer to many printed works. Fortunately, I do not need to specify these individually as they are now included in a work published in 2002. This is *A Nottinghamshire Bibliography: Publications on Nottinghamshire History Before 1998*. Compiled by Michael Brook, this is Volume 42 in the *Thoroton Society Record Series*. Its 8,707 references are indexed by place, subject and author. Where appropriate I have referred to some publications that have been issued since 1998. The bibliography includes a list of institutions holding material from which it was completed. The most accessible of these, for those living in Nottinghamshire, will be the City and County Council Libraries, Nottinghamshire Archives and the two Nottingham University Libraries.

THE FIRST SUBURBS

The plans of Nottingham published from the early 17th century to the middle of the 19th all show a similar shape. Although the borough contained nearly 1,000 acres, stretching five miles from Trent Bridge to Mapperley, the inhabited area was confined to a small part centred around the market place. From north to south this measured about half a mile, from today's Parliament Street to Canal Street. In the opposite direction, from the castle in the west to the border with Sneinton, the distance was about three quarters of a mile, giving an oval shape of about 200 acres.

The reasons for this go back over 1,000 years, beginning in the 6th century when the first Anglo-Saxon settlement was formed. This was on a steep cliff overlooking the flat area south to the River Trent. It was a small area of about 40 acres and was chosen as a burh, an easily defended site. Something of the nature of this site can still be seen in the part of the present city known as the Lace Market. A walk along the foot of the cliff on Cliff Road reveals the sheer face of it, high brick walls erected in the 19th century showing how it had to be shored up. East and west of the Lace Market the site sloped, allowing ditches to be formed. The north side lacked these natural advantages but was defended by the construction later of the town wall.

Like most of the Midland Anglo-Saxon settlements, the burh was surrounded by land which provided the food for the inhabitants, either arable land for growing crops or pasture for grazing animals. This open field system was a communal one, with the land divided into strips allocated to the inhabitants in such a way that each had a share of the differing qualities of soil. In Nottingham two large open fields were the Sand Field to the north-west, separated by a road northwards from the Clay Field to the east. There was also a small field to the

north-west, the Lammas Field. To the south were the meadows, subject to winter flooding from the River Trent, which gave rich alluvial soil as the waters receded.

The western boundary of the burh was another steep cliff, which formed another burh site. This was appreciated by the Normans after 1066 when they built a royal castle there from which to impose their rule. A borough gradually formed to the east of the castle and by early mediaeval times, the twin boroughs had joined up to form the united town which was to remain within the same bounds until the mid-19th century.

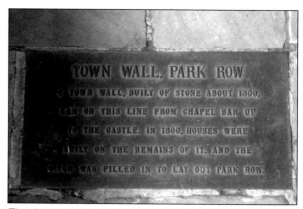

The plaque let into the pavement on Park Row marks the site of the mediaeval town wall, which guarded the town on the north side. Beyond were the Lammas open fields, which were not enclosed until 1840.

The accelerated growth in population in Nottingham from the mid-18th century, due to the industrialisation of the hosiery and later lace trades, resulted in the building of dwellings to house the people. This had to take place within the confines of the mediaeval borough on spare or waste lands, or on gardens and orchards. Building could not take place on the open fields because of opposition from the burgesses. They were by this time a minority of adult men of the borough, forming a closed community. Admission to this body was limited in

One of the first developments following the enclosure was the construction of Regent Street, with handsome tall houses on either side. The layout was designed by architects Hine and Evans and Thomas Chambers Hine's own house is the last one on the west side. A green plaque records this.

earlier times to holders of burgage or house plots and to apprentices who had served their time. They had certain privileges over the open field such as the right to pasture animals, and though they did not necessarily use these themselves, they were permitted to sell their rights to others. They were therefore unwilling to give their consent to allow building on the fields. This was not achieved until after a protracted political struggle, to obtain Enclosure Acts from Parliament. These included payment of compensation to the burgesses, who after 1835 became known as freemen.

The first of these Acts was to allow building on what were known as the Lammas lands. The name was given because the burgesses had the right to turn cattle on to the stubble after the harvesting of crops, celebrated at the Lammas Festival on 1 August. The area was a small one north of Park Row and west of Derby Road and it was laid out in

One of the most original designed houses is this one at the corner of Wellington Circus and College Street. William Parsons, a solicitor and later mayor of Nottingham, owned the house for a time and recorded in his diary how he turfed Wellington Circus in place of cabbages.

The first Albert Hall on North Circus Street was designed by Watson Fothergill, one of Nottingham's finest and most original architects. It was destroyed by fire and replaced by the present building in 1909.

The convent on College Street has been converted into dwellings so the notice on the door no longer applies.

streets is Regent Street, with its large three-storey houses.

Part of this site was allocated for the erection of a Roman Catholic church, St Barnabas, which became a cathedral when the religion was organised into dioceses. The architect was one of the Victorian era's most famous members of the profession, Augustus Welby Northmore Pugin. Another later building was the Albert Hall, built as a concert hall. It later became a Methodist church, and it was rebuilt after a fire. In the 1980s the building was acquired by the City Council and used for cultural purposes. Another hall, on Circus Street, along with some adjoining houses, was demolished in the 1960s and the site was used for the erection of Nottingham Playhouse, in a style which contrasted sharply with its neighbours. It has become nationally famous as one of Britain's regional theatres. The open space in front of the theatre has recently been used to house a modern sculpture, a 'Sky Mirror' of concave shape. An

a planned fashion with a circular enclosure in the centre, which is still there and is known as Wellington Circus. Houses in the area had to be of a high standard of construction, and most are still there. Most of them today are occupied by businesses and offices. One of the most imposing

The earlier buildings at the bottom of Derby Road have been replaced in recent years. In this picture can be seen the tower of the present Albert Hall and the spire of the Roman Catholic cathedral of St Barnabas, designed by A.W. Pugin.

equally innovative modern building adjoining the cathedral is its hall, with a distinctive flèche.

In 1845 a General Enclosure Act was obtained which dealt with the remaining open fields. This was a measure of planning which was ahead of its time, designed to create a new Nottingham with improved housing standards, a planned layout and open spaces. Something of this can still be seen today, but sadly not all its promises were fulfilled. The workings of the Act are described in the next three sections.

The Sandfield

The area known as the Sandfield stretched north of Parliament Street as far as the borough boundary, with Alfreton Road on the west and Mansfield Road on the east. It was an undulating site sloping down to form a valley before rising again to the

The statue in the Arboretum is of Fergus O'Connor, who was elected as an MP for Nottingham in 1847, the only man ever elected to represent the Chartist Movement, which sought electoral reform.

The Arboretum was set out in the Enclosure Act 1845 to be an open space for the benefit of the inhabitants. It celebrated its 150th anniversary in 2002, after having been renovated and improved.

east. Part of it, from Canning Circus, was taken over for a proprietary cemetery, known as the General Cemetery, in 1836.

The Enclosure Act stipulated that two portions should be allocated as public open spaces. One of

these was the land at the northern end of the field known as The Forest, which had been used as a racecourse and extended westwards into Radford parish. It continued to be used as a racecourse until the 1890s, when it became one of Nottingham's public parks. The other site, almost opposite the bottom end of the General Cemetery, was laid out as the Arboretum by the borough council and opened in 1852.

The rest of the field, which stretched from the northern edge of the built-up part of the town on Parliament Street to Forest Road, and from west to east from Alfreton Road to Sherwood Street, was subject to a plan drawn up by enclosure commissioners. Shakespeare Street and the roads

Taken from the General Cemetery, this view shows the substantial houses on Cromwell Street with industrial buildings behind them.

The name Raleigh Cycles can just be seen above the eaves in this photograph, which was taken before the houses in Raleigh Street, from which the cycle manufacturer took its name, were demolished.

northwards were developed with large houses for the better-off classes. The area to the east of Alfreton Road and north of the General Cemetery had working-class houses and some industrial buildings. A new church, All Saints, was built in

This unusual block of houses on North Sherwood Street was built before Salmon's map of 1861 was surveyed.

1863 and a Wesleyan chapel on Shakespeare Street in 1854. It is now a synagogue. Educational buildings included Nottingham Boys' High School, transferred from Stoney Street to Forest Road, a Girls' High School in a former large house on Arboretum Street and the School of Art, later called the College of Art, now part of Nottingham Trent University. In 1881 the Nottingham University College, which included a Natural History Museum and a Free Library was opened. By the end of the 19th century the Sandfield had entirely disappeared apart from the designated open spaces. A variety of developments had taken place including a Board School, hotels, factories, shops and even Nottingham's first electricity generating station.

By 1945 many of the earlier houses, which were built for families with several children and servants,

The Gordon Boys' Home provided a home, uniform and employment for orphans and others in need. The home later moved from Peel Street to an elegant purpose-built house on Cranmer Street.

Clipstone Avenue is a short, secluded row of houses between Peel Street and Annesley Grove. In 1881 four of the 13 houses on the east side were occupied by nonconformist clergymen.

Now converted into flats, this handsome building on Peel Street was built in the 1920s as the Womens' Hospital, replacing premises in Castle Gate.

had become too large for modern needs. Some of them had already been let to more than one tenant, usually without structural alterations to create self-contained flats. The University College had moved to new premises on the edge of the city and its buildings had been taken over for other further education purposes – technical college, college of advanced technology, polytechnic and finally Nottingham Trent University. The latter has expanded by acquiring properties, demolishing them and building new premises. It now occupies a major proportion of the southern part of the former

Sandfield, centred on Shakespeare Street and Goldsmith Street.

The two high schools have followed a similar policy, although on a smaller scale. Demolition of some of the houses has resulted in new properties being built on the sites, and factories and even the modern Women's Hospital on Peel Street have been converted into flats.

The Clayfield

The Clayfield was a much larger area than the Sandfield and it extended from Mansfield Road eastwards to the boundary with Sneinton and northwards as far as the Hungerhills and the boundary with Basford. The land sloped steeply from Woodborough Road, rising again from the valley, which after the enclosure was named St Ann's Well Road. It was so named from the ancient track, which led from the borough to the well. A chapel had been built there in 1409 and the water of the well was said to have healing power. In 1601, the mayor, aldermen and council were ordered to

An engraving done in the 1840s shows the view from the top of Mansfield Road before the Clayfield in the foreground was enclosed.

visit St Ann's Well on Black (Easter) Monday to spend their money with the keeper and woodward. On one occasion King James I visited the well, where he met many of the nobility of the county, who it was reported drank the woodward and his barrels dry.

The enclosure award provided for a public amenity by way of a walk from Woodborough Road in three parts. The first part, Elm Avenue, led to a hill where a reservoir was built and thence

The houses on Curzon Street were of superior design and quality to many of the houses in St Ann's.

along Corporation Oaks as far as Woodborough Road. On the east side of the road the walk was named Robin Hood's Chase, although the apostrophe and 's' have been discontinued.

This area, to become known as St Ann's, was planned in a different manner from the Sandfield. The population of Nottingham, which had been growing each decade from 1801, consisted mainly of workers in the lace and textile trades who required houses. The street plan was based on three major roads

Westminster Street was typical of many streets that led off St Ann's Well Road in having terraces, as can be seen in this photograph.

running north-eastwards: St Ann's Well Road, Blue Bell Hill Road and Carlton Road. A west to east road in the central part was named Alfred Street in three parts – North, Central and South. Radiating from these thoroughfares, usually at right angles in a grid pattern, were the streets of working-class houses, often with terraces leading off them. Factories, workshops and other industrial buildings

Locksley House at the southern end of Robin Hood Chase had been an industrial school for girls, but after being requisitioned during World War Two it was converted into flats.

The track in the centre of this picture led to Hungerhill Gardens from Corporation Road. The building on the left was a police lodge.

The partially demolished houses on Bombay Street in 1971 had been boarded up after the tenants were rehoused to prevent unauthorised occupation.

The knowledge that houses were soon to be demolished led to scenes such as this in Stretten Street.

were built along with the houses, so that the workers did not have far to travel.

Salmon's map of 1861, on a large scale of 1,200 feet to one inch, showed that development had taken place on both sides of St Ann's Well Road, as far as Robin Hood Chase. By the end of the 19th century, the whole area was virtually filled up with high-density housing, along with all other amenities to form a more or less self-contained suburb with churches, chapels, schools, shops, banks, public houses and even a railway station on the Nottingham Suburban Line. Few of the houses had gardens and there was only a small park adjoining the Bath Street burial ground. However, there were the Hungerhill Gardens let out as allotments where the men could grow vegetables as well as roses, for which the gardens became famous, with an annual St Ann's Rose Show.

The north-eastern part of St Ann's Well Road led to Wells Road and Ransom Road, which were less developed and on the edge of what today would be called a green belt. What later became known as the

Coppice Mental Hospital, but was more unfeelingly originally styled as the Lunatic Asylum, stood in its own grounds (now converted into living accommodation).

The beginning of the 20th century saw the introduction of electric trams, including lines through St Ann's. At the southern end of St Ann's Well Road, the Electricity Department built a new generating station to provide power for the trams. As elsewhere in the city, trams gave way to trolley buses and petrol buses. The 1920s and '30s saw an increase in road traffic from motor cars, and the opening of cinemas and dance halls. When the City Council resumed slum clearance in the 1950s, St Ann's was not one of the first areas to be tackled. When its turn came, with the first clearance order in 1967, a different approach to clearing and redevelopment was taken. In the Radford area, particularly in the late 1950s, the policy had been to demolish unfit houses but to leave the more expensive public houses and industrial buildings. In St Ann's a much more radical approach was adopted, to demolish a much greater proportion of the buildings in the area. The redevelopment, mainly housing at a lower density than the old layout, meant that the street pattern was altered. Although main thoroughfares were retained, many of the old grid-plan streets disappeared. This allowed new housing to be in groups which were separated from all but essential traffic.

To achieve this extensive alteration it was necessary to carry it out over a period. The compulsory purchase orders were introduced in 11 phases over a period of six years. The area covered was 264 acres and the number of properties was 9,635 at a cost of £5¼ million pounds. It involved the re-housing of 30,000 people

and this naturally meant a great deal of planning and co-ordination. It was not possible, in the early stages at least, for those who were rehoused to be found accommodation in the St Ann's area. They were moved to other council estates throughout the city.

The scheme was not without its critics. Some considered that some of the older houses could have been retained and improved. An organisation called SATRA (St Ann's Tenants and Residents Association) was formed to provide a means for those affected to have a voice.

Many, particularly older people who had lived in St Ann's all their lives, regretted the loss of the neighbourliness which had existed in the closely-packed dwellings. Others, the younger ones, welcomed the move from cramped houses without modern amenities to new ones with central heating, gardens, bathrooms and space for refrigerators and washing machines.

St Ann's, like other parts of Nottingham's inner city, was not immune to some of the national problems of the latter part of the 20th century. Increased crime, violence, drug taking and dealing have probably been no worse in St Ann's than in some other areas, but because of the physical layout of the estate, the City Council has in recent years taken measures to increase security.

Cranmer Street today has some of the redeveloped houses on the left, opposite the former Gordon Boys' Home.

The Meadows

When the invaders from across the North Sea sailed up the River Humber and the River Trent, they selected a site on a cliff to establish a burh, or borough, which they named Snotingeham, later altered by the Normans to Nottingham. The burh could be more easily defended on a hill than on a flat site, so the cliff was probably the main reason for selecting Nottingham. The site, a small area around what centuries later became the Lace Market, was about a mile from the River Trent. While the Anglo-Saxons appreciated the river as a means of communication, as a source of water and of fish for food, they probably realised that from time to time the river would flood.

The burh needed agricultural land around it and the land between it and the river would supplement the two other large tracts to the north. Because of its liability to flood it was suitable for both arable and pasture, and has ever since been known just as the meadows, the name later being dignified by a capital letter 'M'.

A burh's inhabitants formed themselves into a community, with the adults who obtained freehold sites for houses, or burgages, having certain rights as burgesses which other inhabitants did not. These included the right to have a share in the open fields to grow crops and pasture animals. They also had the right, after crops had been harvested, to use the fields for grazing. To protect these rights, and also to maintain law and order in the town, the burgesses became a governing body, with rights and privileges (and some duties) granted by charters. This body eventually became a council, with aldermen, councillors, sheriffs, a mayor and various officers.

Although records of the affairs of the councils go back in some cases to the early mediaeval period, the earliest surviving written records about the management of the open fields begin in the 16th century. One of these was a report of the Mickletorn Jury in 1553. This was a kind of watchdog body that inspected the town from time to time, looking out for any infringements of the rules governing the town. On the 27 April 1553, part of a long report to the mayor and council claimed that some were putting more than eight cattle on the meadows, contrary to the regulations. Other complaints included the fact that some were putting scabbed and diseased horses in the meadows, affecting other animals. The council also protected the meadows after poor summers by postponing the date when the meadows could be thrown open to grazing. If they found burgesses were abusing their privileges by putting in animals belonging to non-burgesses, they could withdraw the status of burgess.

By the end of the 18th century Nottingham had started to become industrialised and the population had increased. The number of burgesses remained more or less the same, as there were restrictions governing who could become one. They were,

This photograph, taken in 1906, shows a wall separating two halves of Bathley Street. The City Council wanted to demolish it but the trustees of St Gabriel's Church claimed it was on their property. The council made a compulsory purchase order and demolished the wall.

therefore, a minority of the townspeople, and although most of them no longer exercised their rights in the meadows, they could always sell them to farmers and others who could use them. At the same time there was a growing opposition to the burgesses' refusal to allow building to take place on the open fields. This became more serious as the town expanded, as it could only do so within the ancient limits of the built-up area. However, the Corporation – the mayor, sheriffs, aldermen and other officers – was still a closed body that was not elected by the townspeople as a whole.

The situation was changed in 1835 when an Act of Parliament reformed all borough councils, making them subject to more democratic elections. This led to a successful campaign to allow building on the open fields by obtaining a general Enclosure Act in 1845. The Act had some novel features and laid down regulations about the way development was to take place. The details had to be settled by an independent commission, which had to draw up an award allocating land-ownership. In the Meadows, as it now became known as a suburb, the commissioners set out provisions for open spaces, to consist of a 90ft-wide walk from Queens Road to Wilford Ferry and a cricket ground of 9 acres. The commissioners also had to draw up a plan showing how the street pattern in the Meadows would be arranged.

The northern edge of the Meadows had been separated from the town since 1794 by the Nottingham Canal and then in the 1830s by the Midland Railway. The main road from Trent Bridge was the Flood Road, later to be called London Road, to the east side of the town. With the establishment of a railway station on the south bank of the canal, a bridge was built in 1842 on Carrington Street. The commissioners extended this road to the Trent Bridge with a new Arkwright Street, with other streets running off it to the east and west. The old footpath on the west side was made into a proper road with a bridge over the canal.

A plan of the town drawn up between 1851 and 1861 showed how far the development of the Meadows had gone. The area was more restricted than what later became developed because on the west and south sides were the King's Meadow, still extra-parochial and outside the borough, and Wilford parish, part of which was north of the River Trent. The plan showed the main group of houses to be off Kirkewhite Street, as far as Mayfield Grove, with two small groups near to London Road. Arkwright Street was only developed as far as the site for St Saviour's Church, built in 1864. The houses are shown to be close together in terraces and despite the provisions for housing standards in the Enclosure Act some builders managed to build sub-standard dwellings, including some below the flood level.

Development proceeded apace, with industrial premises adjoining houses. The extension of the borough in 1877 enabled the former Kings Meadow area and North Wilford to be built on. The latter had seen Clifton Colliery opened in 1870,

The rear of Burton's almshouses on London Road before they were demolished. A new almshouse block was erected in the Meadows.

This view of St Saviour's Church and shops on Arkwright Street was taken after properties on Glebe Street had been demolished.

London Road and Nottingham Canal before demolition in 1962, showing some of the larger houses.

with houses for workers nearby. By 1881 Arkwright Street, Wilford Road, Crocus Street, Waterway Street and Kirkewhite Street were all completely built up with minor streets and terraces leading off them. Crocus Street was poor compensation for the loss of the fields of crocuses for which the Meadows of old were famed. Mrs Ann Gilbert, who died in 1866, lived to see the transformation, which she described in a poem, *The Last Dying Speech of the Crocuses*:

> Spirit of giant trade! we go; on wings of night
>   we fly,
> Some far sequestered spot to seek where loom
>   shall never fly,
> Come line and rule – come board and brick –
>   all dismal things in one –
> Dread Spirit of Inclosure come – thy wretched
>   will be done!

The face of the Meadows was altered in two ways towards the end of the 19th century. The Great Central Railway crossed Queens Road, Waterway Street and Arkwright Street in quick succession, with a station reached up steps. From there it pursued its way on embankments and viaducts to cross the River Trent at Wilford. The railway company built houses for its workers, one section of which was Glapton Road, with six terraces named after places beginning with the first six letters of the alphabet. They are still there and of sufficiently good construction to be successfully modernised. Other buildings in this area which are still there were built on the former North Wilford parish.

The second, and redeeming, feature of this period was the building of the Victoria Embankment, a mile long from Trent Bridge to Wilford Toll bridge. This was to be of some benefit, for a time at least, as a flood prevention measure. It also helped ensure the preservation of the adjoining open space for sports.

Some superior detached houses were built at the eastern end of the Embankment. This area had been the site of the Nottingham Waterworks Company's reservoir and pumping station, which had been used to supply water from the river to the town. The company was taken over by the Corporation Water Department, which built new reservoirs elsewhere. What was described as the waterworks estate was then developed with new streets from Turney Street southwards.

An ordnance survey map of 1899 shows that the Meadows from Turney Street northwards was almost completely built up. It also shows the tram track from the town as far as Trent Bridge. This was however, the track for horse trams, and the tram stables are shown on Muskham Street. Shortly afterwards the electric trams were introduced and the stables were demolished. Also shown on this map are what were then the newly erected Mundella and Colleygate Schools, which were then surrounded by unbuilt-on land. A few years later a new church, St Faith's, was built nearby.

An important development during World War One was the construction of a large new factory on Kings Meadow Road by the firm of Cammell Laird. This was used for making munitions. After the war a programme of building council houses in the Meadows on the vacant land south of Holgate Road began. This was followed by the erection of a war memorial in the form of a triumphal arch with wrought iron gates on the Victoria Embankment, which led to an ornamental rock garden.

In 1932 the Meadows, along with West Bridgford and Wilford, suffered severe flooding from the River Trent due to heavy rain. Floods were nothing new, as notches with dates carved on a high wall adjoining Trent Bridge showed how high previous floods had risen. An enterprising printer published an eight-page booklet entitled *Souvenir of the Great Flood, May 1932* with photographs. One of those showed how the floods had spread through the Meadows as far as the Midland Station. The appropriate authorities all agreed that something should be done to prevent a repetition.

The River Trent in summer continued to be a pleasant resort, especially on Bank Holidays when thousands of people thronged the Embankment, where deck chairs were hired out. Trips by boat to either Wilford or Colwick were a popular feature, regattas were held and swimming races were officially permitted. The Corporation had erected a bathing shed upstream by screening off part of the

A house on Bruce Grove was rather more architecturally distinguished than most of the Meadows houses.

Embankment so that the bathers (men and boys only) could change on payment of one penny.

Prior to World War One there seems to have been little in the way of entertainment and culture in the Meadows apart from 28 public houses. For other entertainment Nottingham was near enough for people to walk to for theatres or music halls, or for more refined tastes visits to the Castle Museum and Art Gallery and the Central Public Library. The years just before the war saw the coming of the district's first two cinemas. The Midland Picture Palace near the junction of Arkwright Street and Queens Road was converted from a motor garage and later named the Queens. At the other end of Arkwright Street the Globe was a new building which was the first sight to greet people coming into Nottingham over Trent Bridge.

In the 1920s the Imperial Cinema was erected on Wilford Road and 10 years later the Grove, one of

Bunbury Street, with terraces leading off on both sides, was one of the first to be cleared in the 1970s.

the more modern cinemas suitable for talking films, appeared. The Corporation had started to provide amenities by erecting the public swimming baths and wash house on Muskham Street and a public library on Wilford Grove in an attractive style.

The Meadows suffered some damage in World War Two from enemy air raids, just as it did in the first one from zeppelins. The early post-war years were difficult for the people of the Meadows, as elsewhere, because of rationing and a shortage of new goods of all kinds, but for the Meadows these were exacerbated by the disastrous floods of March 1947. These came after a severe winter with the grounds frozen and when the thaw set in the River Trent flooded and reached as far as the Midland Station. A relief fund was set up and payments were made to people in the Meadows who had suffered damage.

As in 1932, the authorities agreed that something should be done to prevent flooding but this time the discussion resulted in action. A sluice

system lower down the river was improved and the embankment on both sides was strengthened. Heavy rains in the autumn of 2001 caused the river level to rise dramatically but the defences held.

In 1952 a rather curious anomaly which affected the boundary of the Meadows and of the city was corrected. A stretch of the southern riverbank on both sides of Trent Bridge had since time immemorial been part of the borough and city. One effect of this had been that the county council started to build a new county hall on Loughborough Road, on a site which was in the city, in 1936. This was altered in 1952 when the boundary became the centre of the river bed, meaning that the city lost half of Trent Bridge.

Arkwright Street had for years been noted as a good local shopping centre. The post-war period was one of changing retail habits, with the coming of supermarkets and shopping malls, and Arkwright Street, like other suburban areas, could not compete with them. Shops closed or were used

The entrance to the Meadows from Trent Bridge has been altered with the disappearance of Arkwright Street.

for other purposes and property deteriorated, making it a 'miserable mile', as it was labelled by its critics. The houses too had suffered from years of neglect, as most of them were rented from landlords who could only afford basic repairs.

The creating of clearance areas in the Meadows in the 1970s came as an opportunity to create a modern Meadows. Most of the older houses were unfit and were demolished, as were other properties, such as public houses, factories and workshops, which were deemed to be in the way of the planned redevelopment. An essential feature of this was to separate the replacement housing from through traffic. To this end Arkwright Street and Wilford Road were eliminated, apart from small stretches at the northern end. In their place new roads were constructed. A new road, Meadows Way, ran parallel with London Road for about a quarter of a mile separated by only a few yards. On this space a grass bank was raised and planted with saplings and daffodil bulbs. The bank was designed to reduce the traffic noise. At the time pessimists foretold the destruction of the saplings, especially as the route led from the railway station, from which football supporters walked to both grounds, which were nearby. Their fears proved groundless and the trees have grown to maturity. On the west side, Wilford Road ran past the Royal Ordnance Factory, which had taken over the Cammell Laird factory on Kings Meadow

Road. Renamed Queen's Drive it then went along the north bank of the River Trent as far as the new bridge over the river, which connected the Clifton Estate in an alternative route to that along Wilford Lane.

In between these two new roads, a further new road called Sheriff's Way and Robin Hood Way provided a route for local traffic, including buses for the newly erected dwellings. There were no high-rise flats, the houses, maisonettes and flats being arranged in blocks with footpath access. The number of replacement dwellings was much lower than those demolished, which resulted in a smaller population. One consequence of this was that one of the three Anglican churches, St Faith's, became redundant and the building was used as an independent school. All the local authority schools in the area were either demolished or used for other purposes. New schools were built, one of which was not only outside the Meadows but was also on the other side of the river.

The new Meadows is visually a more attractive place, with less crowded residential sectors and with the old industry gone and only a small industrial zone on the edge of the district. At the end of 2002 the former Ordnance Factory disappeared and plans for its redevelopment are awaited. The Meadows has its problems but these must be regarded as due to some extent to the general sociological changes of the 20th century.

The industrial buildings to the north of the Meadows on Queens Road have been retained.

PART ONE:
THE INNER SUBURBS

ASPLEY AND CINDERHILL

The history of Aspley up to 1928 is the history of one large house, Aspley Hall. From then onwards Aspley is a Nottingham suburb which is largely a creation by the City Council of a council housing estate. The name at least is much older. It was in Radford parish but at the extreme north tip and until the 19th century was separated from the village by open country. Its earliest mention is as Aspeleia in 1108, and was derived from a word relating to aspen trees and a clearing.

This view of the Aspley estate is dated to the mid-1930s. Melbourne Road is on the right of the picture.

Aspley Hall Cottages on Aspley Lane are the only remaining part of the former Hall estate and were provided for the estate workers.

Dr Thoroton noted that the reversion of rights in Aspley Wood was leased by Edward Southworth, gent, in 1563 to two London merchants. A rental dated about 1554 stated that Southworth had a lease of 21 years. The rental also gives an account of 'Asshepley Halle' belonging to Lady Stanhope, a house 'sore decayed and almost utterly ruined'. It had belonged to the prior and monks of Lenton, who were dispossessed in 1538 by the dissolution of the monasteries. After the house was restored it had various owners. Thoroton stated that Aspley Wood

Hall was the dwelling place of Thomas Blyth in the reign of Queen Elizabeth. It was later occupied by various members of the Willoughby family, some of whom were Catholics. The baptism register of Radford St Peter's church records the baptism of Willoughby children in the early part of the 19th century, the parents' address being given as Aspley Hall.

The Hall was later the home of William Burnside and then Richard Birkin, both of them wealthy Nottingham manufacturers who were able to retire to this country house, as it still was. The last owner

Melbourne Road, the main road through the estate, has retained its wide central grass verge and trees.

The footpath on the north side of Melbourne Road was formerly the track of the mineral railway line from Cinderhill colliery.

was a county alderman, G.E. Taylor, who bought it in 1925 and lived there until he died in 1965. It then remained empty for three years until it was demolished.

On the opposite side of Aspley Lane was St Margaret's Church, built in 1936 as part of the Aspley housing estate. By 1928 the City Council was looking for new sites on which to build more council houses. To enable properly planned estates, the council thought it necessary to acquire large sites, but it could not find suitable ones entirely in the city. There was some undeveloped land on the west side of Old Basford, beyond which were the county districts of Bilborough and Wollaton. The council acquired lands in these areas and proceeded to build council estates, which went beyond the existing boundary. They were able to bring these added areas into the city in 1932 by an extension Act.

The first part of the Aspley Estate consisted of a contract for 1,200 houses on land entirely within the existing boundary. From then on the estate was expanded westwards until 1939. Further houses had begun to be built there when war broke out but not all of them were allowed to be finished. Instead the existing work was 'mothballed' until after the war when they were completed.

The first phase of the estate started at Nuthall Road, bounded in the south ride by a new road, Melbourne Road, a wide road with houses on both sides as far as Aspley Lane, with a grassed area with trees in the centre. The estate then went to the north of Melbourne Road, in a series of concentric circles, the centre one being reserved for schools. An unusual feature on Melbourne Road was a railway level crossing. This was part of a mineral line which had been in existence for nearly 100 years, and was used to haul coal from the nearby Cinderhill Colliery to Nottingham. The crossing was only used a few times each day by trains, supervised by a man with a red flag. The council later managed to have the line closed and the site became used as a footpath, which is still there.

The estate was subsequently expanded until it was more or less a square shape, bounded on the west by Aspley Lane and on the north by Broxtowe Lane. Two schools were built in the centre of the estate, with shops, recreation grounds, nonconformist churches, a library and a cinema, the Forum. This was only the beginning of the expansion of council housing, which extended to the city boundaries of Wollaton, Bilborough and

Napoleon Square is pictured here shortly before demolition in the 1960s.

Two-Miles Houses was a small hamlet on Nuthall Road adjoining Napoleon Square.

Strelley, including the area of Broxtowe (see separate chapter).

Cinderhill, where the railway line from the colliery started, is shown on a map of 1775 as Cinder Hill, so called because of the residue from lime burning kilns. It was a small hamlet in Basford parish, adjoining Nuthall and Bulwell. In 1841 Thomas North, who already owned collieries nearby, started to sink a new colliery to be known as Cinderhill, although its shafts and surface buildings were in Nuthall parish. The adjoining hamlet in Basford parish was increased by North's provisions for the miners. He built 53 dwellings in Napoleon Square, off Broxtowe Lane, and 34 and a Baptist mission in Holden Square. He also paid for a new Anglican church, Christ Church, costing £2,000 on

land given by the Duke of Newcastle. T.C. Hine, the Nottingham architect, designed the church. North was a councillor on Nottingham Town Council and mayor in 1844. He was a man of great initiative but he became too ambitious in his enterprises and when he died the value of his estate was offset by debt. The Wright family were able to acquire Cinderhill Colliery and renamed it Babbington.

Commercial buildings are being erected on Phoenix Park, the site of the former Cinderhill (later named Babbington) colliery.

With the annexation of Basford parish by the borough in 1877, the identity of Cinderhill became less defined as it gradually merged more closely with Basford.

Cinderhill Colliery continued to be successful but an adjoining one, Newcastle Colliery, was less so and closed in 1928. The separate identities of this part of Basford started to disappear in the 20th century. The building of one of the first council housing estates at Stockhill was followed by the expansion of the Aspley, Broxtowe and Bells Lane area to form a more or less combined suburb. Thomas North's Napoleon Square survived until the 1960s when it was acquired by the city and the houses demolished. A new development on the site is Keverne Close.

The former hamlet of Cinderhill has been transformed in the second

The Elms, a large house on Nuthall Road, has survived the redevelopment surrounding it.

Basford Hall was built by the Edge family and was occupied in its early days by Thomas North, the colliery proprietor.

half of the century. A curious feature was a short stretch of road called Dark Lane. This was a private route for the 'Ripley Rattler' the tramway which ran from Nottingham to Ripley until it ceased in the 1930s. Just to the north of the Red Lion public house is Basford Hall, a large mansion occupied at one time by Thomas North. It was more recently converted into a Miner's Welfare social club, but with the closure of Cinderhill Colliery it is now used as offices. Adjoining Basford Hall is a new further education campus. The rest of the site to the west of Basford Hall formerly had a large pond. This has been drained and a large hotel and restaurant built on the site. The demolition of the Cinderhill Colliery buildings has seen the creation of a new Phoenix Park, with business premises and a 'park and ride' bus terminal.

BASFORD

Basford was one of four Anglo-Saxon settlements which were founded near the River Leen and which later became part of the adjacent borough of Nottingham. The Leen, a small tributary of the River Trent, starts at Newstead some eight miles north of Nottingham. It flows southwards more or less in a half circle, past the borough (now a city) and into the Trent. The four settlements all had names which indicated that they had chosen their situations to be close to a supply of water. In Basford's name the name is believed to be from 'Bassa', a personal name and a ford.

When established as an ecclesiastical parish it was a large one, 2,893 acres, and stretched for two and a quarter miles from west to east and one and half miles from north to south. Most of it was fairly

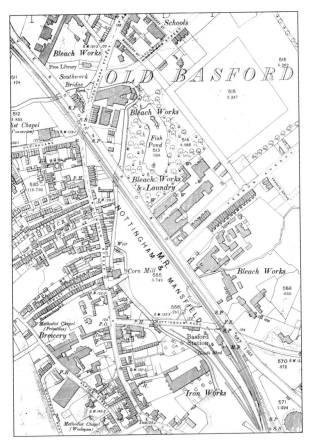

This part of the Basford Workhouse still survives as part of the Highbury Hospital.

flat apart from the eastern side, where it rises steeply to its border with the borough at what later became Mapperley. In the Domesday Book there were five manors, which contained meadows, woodlands, five mills and a priest. Although a priest is mentioned, there is no mention of a church. One was founded after the Normans came to England in 1127 by Robert of Basford, one of the followers of William, Duke of Normandy, who was rewarded with grants of land in England. The church was dedicated to St Leodegarius, a French saint who was martyred in the seventh century.

There is little known of what life was like in the centuries after the conquest up to the 17th century, but no doubt it was little different from other similar communities. In 1676 Dr Robert Thoroton published his *Antiquities of Nottingham* and writes that in Basford Town there were 12 owners of land, whom he named, together with others. He would have obtained this information from a survey of

Sherwood Forest by Richard Bankes, Basford being part of the royal mediaeval forest. The survey, with maps, has recently been published by the Thoroton Society of Nottinghamshire. It shows that there were 18 freeholders, none of whom had substantial holdings, 60 acres being the largest.

The map shows that over half of Basford, some 1,567 acres, was common land. One large area of 1,205 acres occupied most of the central and eastern parts of the parish. This land, described as waste land, would probably have been used mainly for grazing cattle rather than growing crops. It would have provided the villagers with wood for fuel and rabbits for the pot as well. The 1609 map shows that most of the houses were near the Leen, where the mills would have provided work.

Some idea of the size of the population in the 17th century is provided for by two sources. The Protestation Return of 1641 was drawn up for men of 18 years and over to affirm their allegiance to King Charles I. It also gives us some idea of the composition of the population. There were 88 adult men, and as this includes names occurring more than once, there were no doubt some sons living with parents. This could mean a total population of about 350 people living in 70 or so houses.

Thirty-three years later another document, which has survived, is a Hearth Tax return. This listed the names of the people who paid this tax, at a rate for each hearth in the house. There were 63

Situated at the corner of Basford Road (formerly High Street) and Whitemoor Road was this house with stylish window surrounds and doorway.

houses at Basford, again giving a population similar to that in 1641. By 1801 when the first National Census was taken Basford's population had risen to 2,124. This increase in population was matched by most of the villages near Nottingham, which itself had seen an increase from about 5,000 prior to 1750, to nearly 30,000.

These increases were mainly due to industrialisation of hosiery manufacture. This was not, as in Lancashire and Yorkshire, a factory-based industry, but used the stocking-frame. This invention of the 16th century was developed, as its name implies, for making stockings at a greater speed than knitting by hand. The frames, often operated in the homes of the people, were later adapted to make other garments and, in time, for machine-made lace.

Another 'revolution' took place in the 18th century, which altered both ways of life and the appearance of the countryside. This was the agrarian or agricultural revolution, which made agriculture more efficient in two ways. One was the scientific study of crops and the other the changing of the old open field systems or strip farming, to hedged fields under what were known as the Enclosure Acts.

This affected Basford late in the 18th century with 'An Act of Parliament for dividing and enclosing the open fields, meadows, forest,

commons and waste lands within the parish of Basford'. The Act was passed in 1792 and had been petitioned for by owners of land there, including the Duke of Newcastle, Ichabod Wright and Jeffrey Brook. Commissioners were appointed to carry out the provisions of the Act by allocating appropriate parts of the common lands to the various owners and drawing up a map to show where roads were to be made. The enclosure affected nearly 1,500 acres of land on the east side of the parish and in the following century they were developed with building, creating the new suburbs of Carrington, Sherwood and Mapperley Park. These are dealt with in separate chapters.

The early years of the 19th century were troubled ones for England, the Napoleonic Wars causing economic difficulties. In the East Midlands the stocking frame industry was declining, as it could not compete with the steam-powered textile mills of Lancashire and Yorkshire. Technical changes to try to increase production were opposed by the workers and in Basford this led to violence involving machine breaking, as in other villages. In Basford in 1811 various workshops were attacked and about 30 frames destroyed. For this two men were sentenced to 14 years transportation.

Ever since the start of the 17th century each parish was responsible for looking after those unable to do so themselves. This included the sick, infirm, aged and orphans or abandoned children.

The small street off Whitemoor Road no longer lived up to its name, Pleasant Place, in the 1960s. It was later cleared.

The railway and later Vernon Road meant that Church Street, Old Basford, retained its quiet atmosphere. The building on the right was the former National School and was demolished in the 1960s.

Assistance could be by payment of money or by admittance to institutions known as poor houses or workhouses. With the rapidly increasing population and industrialisation, the Poor Law system, as it was called, was becoming increasingly unworkable at the end of the 18th century, especially in large towns. In 1814 Basford became the centre of one of the methods being tried to improve the situation. A body known as a Poor Law Incorporation was established to administer the systems over a large number of villages within a 10-mile or so radius around Basford. A workhouse was built on the northern boundary of the parish, adjoining Bulwell, in which all those in the area covered could be housed if necessary. Twenty years later a national system on similar lines was set up, known as the New Poor Law. Unions of parishes were subject to the administrations of Boards of Guardians and the Basford Guardians was one such body. It remained in existence, as did all the Guardians, until 1931. The site at Basford expanded to include a hospital,

then became the responsibility of Nottinghamshire County Council and the site, with some of the earliest buildings, is now Highbury Hospital.

The first quarter of the 19th century saw changes in Nottingham and the surrounding area in the textile trades. The decline in the hosiery trade based on the stocking frame continued but was offset by the beginning of lace manufacture on newly developed machines. The population of the parish of Basford benefited from this and had risen to 6,305 at the 1831 census. *White's Directory* of 1832 refers to this as 'great augmentation, which had resulted in several new villages being built in the parish, which now contain seven bleaching establishments, five corn mills and several hundred stocking frames and bobbin net machines'. One of these new villages, about a mile south of the old village, became known as New Basford and is described in a separate chapter.

One reason for the growth of population in the adjoining villages was connected with the growth of

The houses and shops on this section of Church Street have all been demolished.

Nottingham itself. During the 18th century it had become an important commercial centre for the region's hosiery trade. Although most of the actual work was done in the village on the stocking frames, other processes had to be carried out in the borough. This included finishing processes such as embroidery, but more important was the selling of the goods, together with the distribution of them and the commercial work such as bookkeeping. This became extended in the first half of the 19th century when the lace trade started to grow, which resulted in Nottingham's population almost doubling by 1851. The houses needed to support this increase had all to be built on whatever space, gardens or orchards, could be found within the confines of the old mediaeval town. Although there was plenty of undeveloped land both north and south of the town, these were the former open fields. The burgesses had certain rights there and for many years refused to allow building on them.

As a result Nottingham had become an overcrowded town, with poor standard houses for most people and little in the way of sanitation. These conditions contributed to the spread of contagious and infectious diseases, including smallpox and cholera. Nottingham was not alone in having such conditions and the government set up a commission to investigate and report on the towns. An inspector, J.R. Martin, stated in his report that Nottingham's conditions were unequalled in misery anywhere else in manufacturing cities.

Mr Martin also visited Basford, where he said that the general state of health was favourable, although the public sewers were of inferior arrangement and construction. He also criticised the common practice of throwing refuse into the streets and the lack of open ground for recreation.

One result of the government's enquiries was the passing of an Act which enabled districts to set up their own Local Boards to control and regulate their

The former Cinderhill Co-operative Society was taken over by its big brother and was later closed when demolition of the houses in the Old Basford clearance area started.

areas. Basford appointed such a board in 1856 and it carried out improvements to highways, instituted street lighting, appointed an inspector of nuisances and opened a cemetery on Nottingham Road.

The appearance of Basford changed markedly in 1848 when the Midland Railway built a line from Nottingham to Mansfield with a station at Basford. A new bridge was built near St Leodegarious's Church and two level crossings and footbridges permitted communication between the two halves that Basford was now divided into. One of the two level crossings still survives. The Gas, Light and Coke Company built Basford Gas Works adjoining the railway.

The continued expansion in population caused concern because of its effect on the River Leen, which became virtually an open sewer for industrial and domestic waste. The four districts all contributed to this, as did the town, so a board was set up in 1871 to remedy this. It was not successful and in 1876 the town council announced that it intended to apply to Parliament for an Act to extend its boundaries. This was to be done by bringing the four Leenside villages and Sneinton, Nottingham Park and North Wilford within the town's boundaries. This was a measure which was also designed to help Nottingham's trade and provide uniform standards throughout the enlarged borough. Basford Local Board, as well as the other

Boards, did not offer much opposition to the proposals and in 1877 the Act created the enlarged borough. It is some measure of the wisdom of this that 20 years later Nottingham was granted city status and had a population of 250,000, becoming one of the principal cities of England.

Basford's first visible benefit of the new regime was the building of Vernon Road, which, together with Radford Road and Highbury Road, opened up a direct link with Nottingham. Another major event was the building of Southwark Street School in 1883 by the Nottingham School Board. The last quarter of the 19th century saw Nottingham's lace trade becoming a worldwide industry and the town and its surrounding districts saw the building of new factories, increasingly powered by steam, warehouses, shops, banks and public buildings and the houses for the workers. Basford played its part in all this, especially Old Basford with its bleaching works.

Communication between Basford and Nottingham was extended by the building of a new railway, the Great Northern, with a station at the junction of Vernon Road and Highbury Road. Horse-drawn buses and trams were superseded in the early years of the 20th century by electric trams. This period also saw the building of a Corporation refuse destructer near the newly erected Northern Baths and the acquisition of land for Vernon Park.

The building of new houses continued on the east side of Vernon Road and led to the opening of a new church, St Aidan's on Arnold Road, in 1905 and a new school, Scotland Place, in 1913. Plans for a cinema resulted in the Vernon Picture House, opened just after the outbreak of World War One in 1914.

The 1920s and 1930s saw considerable changes in the Old Basford area. One of the first large council house estates was built at Stockhill in 1921, followed by Highbury Vale Estate, which was partly in Bulwell. The construction of Valley Road from Nottingham Road to Mansfield was part of an outer ring road scheme and Heathfield

Estate was built on the north side. The ring road scheme was extended in the 1930s when Western Boulevard was constructed, starting at Ilkeston Road. It continued as far as St Leodegarious's Church where a new bridge carried the road over the railway and Fairfax Street joined the scheme by connecting with Valley Road.

A new housing estate called Whitemoor Estate was built at this time, which occupied both sides of Western Boulevard. A smaller housing scheme was built on the north side of Arnold Road, and further along this road a new factory, for the Barlock Typewriter Company, was built. A new road from Arnold Road to Valley Road was named Barlock Road. Only older residents will know why the road was given this name, as the factory has gone. Also at this time Basford Rural District Council acquired Rock House on Bagnall Road as its headquarters.

The west side of Old Basford was developed in the 1920s and 1930s. Bar Lane was made into a wider road and two new schools erected, Ellis for boys and Guildford for girls. At the junction of Bar Lane and Nuthall Road a new cinema for the new 'talking' films was built called the Aspley Cinema, now the Commodore Centre. On the other side of Nuthall Road another new housing estate was built, the Aspley Estate. As this extended into parts of Radford and also across the city boundary, together with Broxtowe, Bilborough and Bells Lane, it is the subject of a separate chapter.

A new form of public transport, the trolley bus, which had overhead wires like the trams, but which did not need a special track, was introduced in Nottingham in 1929, and one of the first routes was from Nottingham along Mansfield Road and Nottingham Road, ending at Vernon Road. Another trolley bus route through Basford was operated by the Midland General Omnibus Company from Nottingham to Ripley, replacing the tram route operated by the Nottinghamshire and Derbyshire Tramway Company. Nottingham's trams stopped in 1936 and were replaced by trolley

This quiet rural scene on Basford Road shows how well-built houses can survive.

buses or petrol buses. Basford had two trolley routes to replace its trams, one from Trent Bridge to Bulwell Market Place and the other from Colwick to Bulwell Hall.

The period after World War Two saw a number of far reaching changes in Old Basford. Like Nottingham and the other suburbs the gradual decline in the lace industry affected its textile trades, especially the bleaching and dyeing industries. The Home Brewery's maltings on Alpine Street closed but later was converted to student living accommodation. Cinderhill Co-operative Society was taken over by the Nottingham Society. The railway line closed to passenger traffic, but remained open for freight and so was able to be restored for passengers as part of the Robin Hood Line from Nottingham to Worksop in the 1990s.

The greatest change in Old Basford started in 1962 when the City Council made a scheme for the clearance and redevelopment of much of the older part. This stretched from Cowley Street to David Lane, and from Percy Street to Lincoln Street. After the buildings had been demolished, a new estate of 322 dwellings and 487 garages was built in a layout which eliminated streets such as Brown's Croft, which connected Lincoln Street and Percy Street. The new dwellings included four 20-storey blocks of flats and others with three to eight storeys in a layout known as deck-access.

This venture had an unfortunate start as shortly after it was completed an explosion took place in a similar high-rise block in London, Ronan Point. This showed that the method of construction was flawed and so the City Council had to strengthen the high-rise blocks at Basford, at considerable expense and inconvenience to the tenants. Worse was to follow, as the deck-access dwellings developed faults which caused dampness and condensation. As a result, all the buildings were demolished and a new estate of traditional dwellings was erected on the site.

The area between David Lane and the boundary with Bulwell, through which the River Leen flowed, has been drained and the river diverted. New houses have been built and a pleasant walkway to Bulwell made. Today Old Basford is a mainly residential area, with only light industry units. It awaits a further change, the Nottingham Express Transit, a modern tramway system which will run parallel to the existing railway line. Already new footbridges over the lines have been built.

There is little in Basford of great antiquity apart from the parish church. There are two houses near the church that are of some architectural merit which have survived. One of them, Basford House, also known as the Manor House, is a brick house of seven bays and two and a half storeys. It has been the home of several families who were well known in their day. One resident, Thomas Langford, born

The Midland Railway divided Old Basford, with the part to the east including these houses on Park Lane, which have all been cleared.

in 1696, was the grandson of George Langford, mayor of Nottingham in 1688. Thomas became a goldsmith and it was said of him that his wealth was such that it would have enabled him to pave the Market Square with gold. He was himself mayor of Nottingham on five occasions between 1733 and 1766. In one of his mayoral years, 1740, he was also high sheriff of the county.

Thomas Langford had a town house in Nottingham but had his country residence at Basford House. He died there in 1768. He was a man of culture as well as a wealthy one. In his will he refers to a quantity of silver plate and 14 Spanish pictures at his house at Basford. He also left £10 for the poor of Basford.

Living in Basford House in 1832 was Thomas Bailey, described as a wine merchant with premises in Nottingham. He was a man of many talents, having earlier been in the silk stocking trade. He unsuccessfully stood as a candidate for Parliament in 1830. He did however pursue a political career and played a part in the campaign that resulted in the Reform Act of 1832, which set up a more democratic House of Commons. After his death in 1856 an obelisk and inscription referring to his efforts was erected in a small cemetery opposite Basford House. The cemetery, now disused, is still there, but sadly the obelisk has disappeared. Bailey became a town councillor in 1836, was the proprietor of a newspaper, the *Nottingham Mercury*, and wrote a history of Nottingham and the county entitled *Annals of Nottinghamshire*. His memory is perpetuated by the nearby Bailey Street. It is recorded that his proudest achievement was being the father of Philip James Bailey, who wrote his poem *Festus* between 1836 and 1839. This poem became quite famous, although Bailey junior continued to extend the poem for the rest of his life. It finished as a book of 800 pages with 40,000 lines. It used to be a sign of intellectual ability to be able to claim to have read it. A few lines of the poem, which seem to have survived as a quotation, are:

'We live in deeds not years; in thoughts, not breaths; in feelings; not in figures on a dial'.

After Thomas Bailey died Basford House became the home of the Spencer family for almost 100 years. Richard Birch Spencer, the first to occupy it was the clerk to the Basford Guardians and was succeeded in that post by his son, Charles James Spencer. He became the first clerk to Basford Rural District Council, serving it until 1907. Basford House was then occupied until World War Two by two unmarried Spencer daughters. The house was subsequently occupied by a coal merchant and was later used as offices. It is now a Grade II listed building, as is another 18th-century house. This is at the bottom of Bailey Street, known as Church-fields. It was for many years in the first half of the 20th century the home and surgery of a well-known doctor, Charles Hill. It is now a Health Centre.

Another 19th-century resident of Old Basford was to achieve much greater fame, although he only lived in Basford for a few years as a boy. He was Frank Dyson, born in 1868, the son of the Revd Watson Dyson who came to live in Basford when Frank was about five years old.

Some 60 years later a boyhood friend of Frank's recalled their school days. John Hopkin, a city councillor who was sheriff of Nottingham in 1926–7, and Frank had attended a New Basford School known as the old British School on Radford Road. From there Frank Dyson went to Bradford Grammar School and then Cambridge University. After becoming a doctor of science, he became secretary to the Royal Astronomical Society in 1899.

He was made Astronomer Royal in 1910, a post he held until 1933. He was created a knight in 1915 and Knight of the British Empire in 1926. Sir Frank Dyson died in 1939.

BILBOROUGH AND BROXTOWE

Bilborough and Strelley are adjoining parishes and until the 1920s were owned by the Edge family of Strelley. Much of Bilborough's history is therefore contained in the chapter on Strelley and in appearance the two would have been largely similar up to the 19th century.

Like Strelley, Bilborough was an Anglo-Saxon settlement and the suffix – borough – is derived from burh, meaning a defended or fortified place. In Bilborough's case, this was probably because the Domesday Book records that King Edward, the English king before the Norman conquest, had one bovate of land there. This is one of five holdings he had in the manor of Arnold. In 1938 an archaeological excavation revealed that there had been earthworks in a field north of the church which indicated that the site had been excavated. The main entry in the Domesday Book showed that Bilborough in 1086 was part of the extensive lands

This large farmhouse has been demolished, but the nearby St Martin's Church still survives.

In 1957 Bilborough village was still separated from the council houses, which can be seen in the distance.

Opposite the church the old St Martin's cottages have been modernised and form an attractive group.

held by William Peverel. There were nine men mentioned plus eight acres of meadow, so the village must have been about the same size as Strelley.

As at Strelley, the Protestation Return of 1641/2 does not list the names of all the male adults. Instead there is a note which states that when Josias Aldered came to tender the protestation:

'I found in the church yard one Imanuell Knutten Clerk: Frances Hill: Richard Hill: William Tornline and Simion Wightman who shutt the church door or procured it to be shutt against me: and the said William Tornline and Symion (sic) Wightman said publickly they would take nee protestation at mee.'

However, the two Hearth Tax returns, for 1664

and 1674, show that there were only 10 houses, one of which was the manor house with 18 hearths in 1664, then owned by Sir Thomas Smith, and with only 16 in 1674, then owned by George Willoughby Esq.

Dr Thoroton had little to say about Bilborough, as he had dealt with the owners of the land in his chapter on Strelley. John Throsby, who added notes to Thoroton's account in a revised edition in 1790, said Bilborough had open fields and considerable coal works, the latter being 100 yards deep. The open fields were enclosed by an Act of Parliament in 1808. The Nottingham Canal, opened in 1796, ran through Bilborough from Wollaton and an arm branched off for about half a mile. It ended in what was then Shepherd's Wood. The wood has long since gone and the wharf where the arm ended was somewhere near today's Glenbrook Primary School. The arm of the canal was paid for by the local landowners, the Edges of Strelley and the Willoughbys of Wollaton. The wharf was connected by tram-road to Bilborough and Strelley collieries. Part of it was filled in by 1818 and the rest had ceased to be used by 1874.

The land at Bilborough continued to be used for agriculture until the 1930s, the extensive coal beds beneath the soil being worked from Cinderhill Colliery. In 1901, the census records that the population was 202. Of these 36 were farmers and 17 were colliers. The latter would have been employed at either Broxtowe or Cinderhill collieries. Samuel Pursglove, a widower aged 57,

The Farm House is now used as a community centre. It is only a hundred yards away from the busy Strelley Road.

The post-1946 new Bilborough estate has several types of non-traditional houses, including these BISF houses.

lived in the school house, the school having been founded in 1872. He had two adult daughters and three adult sons living with him. The sons' occupations were bank clerk, demonstrator in chemistry and lithographic printer. They would of course have worked in nearby Nottingham and there were other early commuters in the village – another bank clerk, a mechanical engineer, a warehouseman, and a 17-year-old girl who was a tobacco worker. John Player's factory was about two miles away in Radford.

Broxtowe Colliery was situated at the eastern edge of the parish and is mentioned along with other collieries started by Thomas North in the chapter on Cinderhill. Broxtowe, spelled Brochelestou in the Domesday Book, is listed under three different owners. The King had one bovate, William Peverel had five acres, which were attached to its neighbour Nuthall, and Robert son of William had a small part with one plough and one villager. The name Broxtowe, meaning 'stow, the place of Brocwulf' was not attached to a village but was the name of one of the county's wapentakes. These were divisions of the shire, sometimes described as hundreds. They were meetings, possibly of 100 men of a given locality, who met to discuss matters of common interest. They met out of doors at a spot marked by some physical feature. Broxtowe wapentake in the Domesday Book contained 46 places stretching from Mansfield in the north to the

River Trent and a detached portion on the Leicestershire border. Dr Thoroton stated that it had been in ownership of the Byron, Stanhope and Parkins families, the latter selling it to Thomas Smith, 'who builded the House and adorned the seat'. It was in Thoroton's time it was owned by Sir Francis Top.

John Throsby in 1790 added little to Thoroton's account. He wrote 'The House or Hall here, in some parts, appears ancient, but it is patched with some ordinary and modern buildings. It is rather prettily embowered with trees. I have given but a very slight sketch of it, as a place of little more consequence than giving name to the Wapenlake.'

An industrial estate on Glaisdale Drive has this innovative warehouse design.

A recent study of papers in the Public Record Office published in *Transactions of The Thoroton Society, Volume 100* reveals that Broxtowe Hall was occupied as a garrison for Parliamentarians from 1642 to 1646. A Royalist account of the way the Parliamentary forces left Broxtowe Hall said that near Broxtowe their men so straggled that one party of them met another party in a lane, but thought they were Royalists and fired on them, killing one of their own lieutenants.

In 1937 Nottingham City Council acquired the land at Broxtowe, including the Hall, which was demolished, and built Broxtowe housing estate. Although it was not possible to excavate the site thoroughly, sufficient excavation took place to reveal that the site had been enclosed by an

When John Throsby added to Dr Thoroton's *Antiquities of Nottinghamshire* in 1790, he wrote that he had made a 'very slight sketch of Broxtowe Hall, as a place of little more consequence than giving home to the wapenlake'.

earthwork of Iron Age type and pottery and coins indicated that Roman occupation had taken place.

Both Bilborough and Broxtowe were incorporated into the City of Nottingham from 1932. In 1974, when local government was reorganised, urban and rural district councils were abolished and in their place district councils were established covering much larger areas. One of these, with headquarters at Beeston, consisted of an area of south-west Nottinghamshire north of the River Trent, which had been part of Broxtowe wapentake. The district councils in Nottinghamshire were given new names based on their historic boundaries and so Broxtowe District Council was born. Scope for confusion existed with Broxtowe estate being just over the border in the city.

The lands at Bilborough and Wollaton purchased by the city in the 1930s also became sites for building council houses. One estate was built in the area between Denewood Crescent and Beechdale Road. Further development had to wait until World War Two was over. In 1944 the government announced a new scheme under which it provided pre-fabricated aluminium bungalows for local authorities. These were factory-built and could be provided much quicker than the traditional method of building with bricks. The government was anxious to make sure that accom-

modation would be available for demobilised servicemen. From May 1945, when the European War ended, demobilisation started. Nottingham decided to have 1,000 of these 'temporary' bungalows, which became known as pre-fabs. They were called temporary bungalows as their life was estimated to be only 10 years. In fact most of them were to last much longer, some as long as 50 years. A feature of these bungalows was that each had a refrigerator, as the design did not include a food store.

The majority of these 'pre-fabs' were erected at Bilborough, one large site being oval in shape and situated between Beechdale Road and Wigman Road. These were eventually replaced with more permanent structures on the foundations of the temporary ones. From 1945 another method of speeding up the erection of council houses was the use of non-traditional methods. This too involved factory-made components, which could be erected without using bricklayers. The new methods were used mainly at Bilborough and included BISF (British Iron and Steel Federation), Tarrand Newland and No Fines houses. The latter used a system of erecting, shuttering and pouring concrete to form walls. Large numbers of this type were also built at Clifton. Another innovation at Bilborough was a scheme of 250 permanent aluminium bungalows for miners.

Fortunately, a later artist made a much more romantic painting of the Hall, which was demolished in 1938. (LSL)

This was formulated by the Government to encourage mining areas to increase production of coal in the years immediately following 1945. The council did not necessarily have to allocate every one of these dwellings to miners, provided they could show that they had given preference to housing miners elsewhere in the city. The bungalows were similar to the temporary bungalows but had thicker walls and are still occupied.

The large-scale development of houses at Bilborough, which later also used traditional brick-built houses, was of course accompanied by other amenities. Shops, schools, public houses, a warden-aided scheme for elderly people, open spaces, parks and a swimming bath were provided. On Glaisdale Drive, an industrial estate with modern buildings was laid out for works and warehouses. Between Beechdale Road and the city boundary on Bilborough Road a new suburb of about 1,600 acres was created.

BULWELL

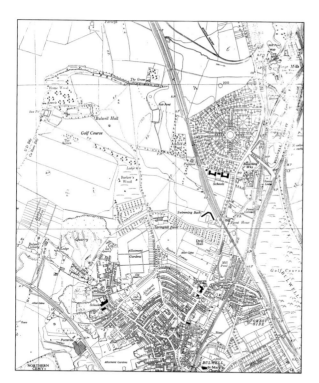

The derivation of the name, according to legend, is that it was from a spring or well, which was started by a bull whose horns struck a large rock from which water flowed. The more prosaic explanation by place-name experts is that the first part is an Anglo-Saxon personal name.

Bulwell was one of the Anglo-Saxon settlements adjacent to the River Leen that was brought within the borough boundary in 1877. Unlike the other Leen settlements, it did not have a common boundary with the borough. Another distinction was that it was part of Sherwood Forest, a royal domain from Norman times. It was among William Peverel's many land holdings after 1066, in place of the English Godric. The Crown also had holdings which gave Bulwell certain advantages.

In the Domesday Book, there were two entries for what was later one district, one for Bulwell and one for Hempshill, which bordered on Nuthall. Taken together they had only six ploughs and only eight men are mentioned. It appears to have been reduced in value since Saxon times when it was valued at 12 shillings, since it is only assumed to be worth five shillings in 1086.

One manor was granted by King John to Philip Marc, who was the sheriff of Nottinghamshire and Derbyshire. He was not a popular man and the nobles who drew up Magna Carta included a clause insisting that he and his nephew and brother be removed from their lands. However, this was not done and he carried on as sheriff until he died in 1224. Dr Thoroton recorded that because of the royal favour that Bulwell enjoyed it had 'a kind of Corporation', having its own courts with its own stewards. It was also allowed to maintain the custom of owning land by copy-hold, under which title to land was proved by entry on the court rolls.

In 1609 a survey of the whole of Sherwood Forest was made, giving details of the occupancy of all lands, which were numbered and shown on a map. Bulwell had 22 plots, most of them small, but 349 acres in three large fields were common to the inhabitants, who thereby had grazing and other rights. There were two large holdings, one belonging to Sir John Byron, 326 acres known as Bulwell Park, which until the dissolution of the monasteries by Henry VIII had been owned by Newstead Priory. The other was the 74 acres of John Strelley, at Hempshill.

The survey map shows how the village houses were all on the banks of the River Leen. This would have been a good source of water supply and fish, and also provided motive power for water-driven

Erected in 1889, but in a mediaeval style, this building can be found in Bank Yard, just off the market place.

One of the oldest buildings in Bulwell is this dovecote, which until a few years ago was hidden away and in poor condition. It has since been repaired.

mills. The survey itself gives details of 22 separate holdings, one of which was owned by Richard Briggs, who had a tenant named Francis Bigg and a water mill.

Some 32 years after the survey, in 1641 another document, which has survived and been transcribed, was produced. All adult men in every parish were asked to sign the Protestation Return, 'protesting' their allegiance to the King. Most of them did and in Bulwell 65 signed, with 52 different surnames. Although Matthew Aynsworth, it is stated, 'hath not taken it'. The Rector Matthew Laycook was 'absent in respect of sickness'. Some of those who signed included Edward Ayscough Esq., James and John Ayscough, both described as 'gent', as was Ferdinando Babington, who was also churchwarden. Another name was Thomas Huckerby, a surname which is still current in and around Nottingham – 20 entries appearing in the

Another old building, erected in 1811, was the former Methodist church on Hazel Street. It was demolished as part of the clearance campaign.

The market place proved to be a useful turning point for the electric trams. Presumably the postcard was based on a photograph, but where are the tram lines and overhead wires?

current telephone directory, two of them in Bulwell. Somewhat surprisingly there are no surnames in the Protestation Return which were present 32 years earlier in the 1609 survey, but of course life expectancy was not as long in those days.

Another source of the names of people living in Bulwell in the 17th century are the Hearth Tax returns, which show how many hearths were in each house. Returns for 1664 and 1674 have been transcribed, but unfortunately the list for 1664 is incomplete. The 1674 document reveals that the occupiers of 30 houses had to pay Hearth Tax, although there is no list of those who were too poor to be chargeable. The return shows that, somewhat

unusually, 14 had only one hearth, with 10 having two or three. One man had seven, and he is described 'Mr ....', his surname being illegible. Those who had four and five hearths are prefixed 'Mr', William Medlow and Mr Newton.

The 17th century saw the erection of a building in Bulwell which still survives and is almost certainly the oldest building in the suburb today. This is the Old Grammar School, a Free School, which was paid for by George Strelley of Hempshill in 1667. The deed which endowed the school stated that it was for 'the educating and teaching of young children of the Inhabitants of the Parish of Bulwell.' The benefactor also provided the school with money to pay a salary for a teacher and to maintain the building. He also laid down rules for running the school, which was limited to 30 pupils. The catechism was to be taught, a chapter of the Bible was to be read daily, and the children were 'to be taught Latin and to write, read written hand and to cypher and cast accounts'.

The school remained in use for 200 years until Joseph Calladine, who had been the master for 44 years, died. The building was then used for other purposes and the endowment income provided scholarships of £15 per annum at Nottingham High School for Boys. As the Nottingham to Mansfield Railway line ran through Bulwell from 1848, the holders would have been able to travel by train. The

This striking building is at the rear of the taller building on Highbury Road, known as the Town Hall, but which was not a seat of local government.

population of Bulwell was approaching 4,000 at the time and a National School had just been built. There were four academies listed in a directory of 1864.

The picturesque building, with curved and stepped gables, is now used as a private residence

This short stretch of the old Bulwell Lane from Basford was superseded when Highbury Road was built.

after a period of various commercial use. It is known as Strelley House and is listed as a Grade II building of special interest.

In 1743, all parishes in the diocese of York were asked by the newly appointed Archbishop Herring to complete a questionnaire. These were completed by the clergyman of each parish; in Bulwell's case, the Revd Thomas Beaumont. He reported that there were 59 houses with 73 families and only one dissenter, a woman of the Presbyterian denomination. He also wrote that he lived in Nottingham as 'the parsonage house is mean, the situation damp and low'. He also said he was not able to fulfil his duties as he was indisposed and the previous Archbishop had granted him a dispensation to live elsewhere.

Another important building was erected in around 1770 by John Newton and was known as Bulwell Hall, although the inhabitants of Bulwell referred to it derisively as Pye Wipe Hall. This must not be confused with Bulwell Wood Hall, a much older building owned by the Byron family that was in Hucknall parish. Bulwell Hall later became the property of the Revd Alfred Padley, who became lord of the manor when he purchased the estate in 1827. Although a clergyman, he was not the rector of Bulwell, although he had a font fixed in the entrance to the Hall which he used to baptise children.

Although the 18th century in England brought changes, which transformed the appearance and economy of the country, none of them had much impact on Bulwell. There was no alteration to the old methods of agriculture, no canal, no turnpike roads or steam-powered factories. By 1801 the population had grown from about 300 to 1,585, rather less than Arnold, Basford and Radford. By 1831 it had grown to 2,611 but the other three villages had increased much more rapidly, with a combined population of 20,000. *White's Directory* of 1832 recorded that there were three bleach works, a lace thread mill, three corn mills, several

The most elegant modern building in Bulwell was the Adelphi Cinema, which was demolished a few years ago.

extensive limestone quarries and kilns and a number of stocking frames and bobbin net machines. There was upwards of 1,600 acres of land, all of which was enclosed apart from 120 acres of open forest. There had been a draft Enclosure Bill in 1799 but this did not proceed, so it is likely that the open fields were later enclosed by agreement. The 1832 list of the names of some of the occupations of residents includes eight bobbin net makers, 11 farmers and 15 lime-burners. There were three nonconformist chapels, two Methodist chapels and one Baptist. There were 10 public houses.

A later edition of the directory, in 1864, gave the population as 3,660, still much smaller than the other Leen villages. There were 851 houses and 'the many good inns and shops' were lighted with gas. It also stated that the principal occupation of the inhabitants was the making of silk gloves on stocking frames, by this time a declining industry. The list of names gives 23 hosiery agents (gloves) and three framesmiths. The number employed in the extractive industries included nine lime-burners and stone quarry owners and 11 stone-masons. Bulwell stone was noted for its quality as a building material. A new industry introduced in 1863 was the Bulwell Match Works of Henry Smith and Company, for the manufacture of their new patent safety waterproof matches, the machinery being driven by a 12hp steam engine. Bulwell Hall was now occupied by the Revd Charles Padley, who

succeeded his father as lord of the manor and rector of the church, which was rebuilt in 1850.

The sanitary conditions of villages which had expanded into small towns in the 19th century caused the government to pass an Act of Parliament enabling such localities to set up a Local Board of Health with elected members. Although Bulwell did set up such a board, it was rather late in doing so. Basford, for example, had one from 1862, but Bulwell's only started in 1872. It did not have much time to do anything of note, as Bulwell was incorporated into the Borough of Nottingham in 1877, along with the other adjoining villages.

The proposal by the borough to take this action, which required an Act of Parliament, did require consideration by the Local Board in 1876. After a town's meeting voted to oppose the move, the Board proposed to present a petition against the Bill, but this was never done. This appears to have been because the borough stated that if Bulwell did not want to come into the borough, they were quite happy to withdraw their proposal. This seems to have caused the inhabitants, or at least their leading men, to reflect that it would probably be to Bulwell's advantage to join the borough.

As mentioned in the chapters on Basford and Radford, one of the improvements put in hand by the borough was to create a unified road system from Bentinck Road to Bulwell, in place of unconnected stretches in the three areas. This resulted in one new road, which although in reality was one thoroughfare, had separately named sections: Radford Road, Vernon Road and Highbury Road. The former road from Basford to Bulwell was Bulwell Lane, and a new section from the Basford end was built, Highbury Road. Bulwell Lane still exists and a short section of it can also still be seen, branching off just behind Bulwell Library.

This new road was not only important as a means of communication but also because it opened up land on either side of Highbury Road for

The isolated part of Bulwell known as Blenheim was perhaps so named ironically because, like the 18th-century battlefield, it was a long way from the village. The new industrial estate is much nearer the modern Bulwell.

development. This was necessary as Bulwell's population almost doubled in the last quarter of the 19th century. Several new streets already existed, with a few houses, between what was to be renamed Highbury Road, on the west side as far as the railway. These included Regent Street and Cranmer Street, both of which had to be renamed after 1877, as there were already streets of those names in the borough. Cranmer Street was renamed Latimer Street, appropriately enough as both men were tried for heresy. Other development had also taken place to the north, around the colliery and quarries.

New schools were erected by the Nottingham School Board on Coventry Road in 1877, Quarry Road in 1880 and the first section of Albert Street in 1896. A new district church, St John's, was built on Quarry Road in 1884. There were also, by the end of the century, four nonconformist churches and Quarry Road had a police and fire station, a free library and a reading room. *White's Directory* for 1902 commented that 'Bulwell presents a remarkable contrast to its surroundings only a few years back'.

As elsewhere in the enlarged borough, building plans for all new construction had to be submitted to the borough council for approval and houses had to comply with statutory regulations. Some of the houses erected on the east side of Highbury Road

were of a superior character, with front gardens and Bulwell stone walls, in small groups of named villas, which are still there today. More development took place in the first decade of the 20th century, particularly in the part east of Highbury Road as far as St Albans Road. On the opposite side is Bulwell Common and Bulwell Forest, with former railway stations of those names either side of the open space with its golf links. Another amenity was the newly constructed tram route from Bulwell with trams every six minutes. By 1914, Bulwell had two cinematograph halls ('the pictures') both owned by Edwin Widdowson; the Olympia Variety Palace and the Picture Palace, both on Main Street. Edwin Widdowson and his son of the same name were partners in the family firm of wholesale druggists. They lived next door to each other on Hucknall Lane, in Jesmond House and Forest House.

Bulwell Hall had been the home of the Cooper family after the Revd Charles Padley left, Percy Hartshorne Cooper becoming high sheriff of Nottinghamshire. After him the Hall was purchased by Thomas Hardy, a brewer from Kimberley. When his widow died, Bulwell Hall with its grounds and manorial rights was purchased by Sir Albert Ball, an alderman on the City Council, who later sold it to the council for the same price that he had paid.

After World War One, Bulwell was developed in the 1920s with the building of council houses at Bulwell Hall and Highbury Vale. The remainder of the Bulwell Hall land was laid out in 1925 as a public park, with sports grounds and another golf course. The Hall was used as a sanatorium and school for tubercular children. Trams gave way to trolley buses, with extension as far as the city boundary with Hucknall. One route continued through the city to Trent Bridge and another to Colwick.

The 1920s and 1930s, with their industrial disputes and economic depressions, probably hit Bulwell harder than the rest of Nottingham. The main industries, coal mining, quarrying and hosiery finishing, were all subject to fluctuating conditions and there were no diversified alternatives, so unemployment remained high. There was some expansion of private housing to the east of Bulwell, around Broomhill Road and St Albans Road, but little other development in this period. There were two interesting developments in the leisure sector, both on Hucknall Lane. An open-air swimming pool was built on the north side, while almost opposite was the Adelphi cinema, a modern 'luxury' cinema, in an innovative architectural style. Unfortunately, it has recently been demolished.

After the end of World War Two in 1945, Bulwell probably shared for a time in the employment boom that followed. There was, however, little change in the built environment for 20 years or so, apart from the provision of 154 temporary bungalows in 1945 at Squires Avenue. In 1965 Bulwell's turn to have its older houses cleared came when the City Council approved a compulsory purchase order for most of the area bounded by Highbury Road and the railway, from Deptford Street to Latimer Street. This was the first cleared area to be redeveloped and involved the demolition of all the properties except the Highbury Vale Hotel and the supermarket, formerly the Highbury Cinema.

The new housing was all low rise, with a new street pattern, using some of the former names – Deptford Crescent, Latimer Close. In the years that followed practically the whole of the area west of Coventry Road and north of the Market Place was redeveloped with new housing. Also to the west, much undeveloped land became housing sites, including the Crabtree Farm estate, Snape Wood and the Hempshill Lane area. The new housing, some council, some private development, extended as far as the city boundary.

The redevelopment enabled a new road system to be designed, with peripheral roads by-passing the old central part of the town. This enabled pedestrianisation of Main Street and Commercial Road to be carried out.

New sites for light industry have been allocated and new transport arrangements made. Bulwell has a bus station and the railway line, used only for freight following the 'Beeching axe', was reopened as a passenger route, the Robin Hood Line, from Nottingham to Worksop. The new Nottingham Express Transit, a modern tram system, will go through Bulwell on the first line from Hucknall to Nottingham. It is due to be opened at the end of 2003.

Today, Bulwell is almost completely built-up, with mainly residential areas and light industry. It does have its own two large open spaces, the Hall park and the Forest. It is also surrounded on the north and west by open land, which is unlikely to be developed.

CARRINGTON

The founding of most of Nottingham's suburbs can only be dated approximately to Anglo-Saxon times. The first steps to the creation of Carrington, however, can be ascribed to Monday 28 February 1825. On that date an auction sale of 20,000 square yards or upwards took place at 4.00pm, conducted by Mr Brearly, at the house of Mrs Ward, sign of King George IV in Carlton Street, Nottingham. An advertisement to this effect stated that a valuable freehold estate at Carrington, almost adjoining the town of Nottingham, would be offered in 40 lots of eligible building land.

A plan accompanying the advertisement showed a triangular plot between the road to Hucknall and the Mansfield turnpike road. The apex of the triangle was at the junction of the two roads,

Taken in 1958, this photograph shows the market place, which had long since ceased to operate as a market.

extending northwards for 260 yards to what is today Sherbrooke Road, the two other boundaries being Hucknall Road and Mansfield Road. The 40 plots were all numbered and the plan showed two short streets running from east to west crossed by another street running north-eastwards. In the centre was a small triangle, called 'area' with a pump. This eventually became Carrington Market Place. The streets were later named High Street, Cross Street and South Street. The land was in Basford parish and when it became part of the borough of Nottingham the names had to be altered, because there were already streets with those names in the town. High Street and Cross Street became Birchin Street and Selkirk Street, while South Street became Jenner Street south of the Market Place and Oak Street to the north.

The land had become available for development after the Basford Enclosure Act of 1792 was passed. The Carrington area had been allocated to Robert Smith, who was a direct descendant of Thomas Smith, who started the first country bank in

Nottingham in the late 17th century. In the 18th century the bank had prospered and opened a London office and other banks. This was all done by the descendants of Thomas Smith, several of whom became MP's and have distinguished families down to the present day. Robert Smith sold his holding to Ichabod Wright, a member of another Nottingham banking family, who had also acquired extensive lands under the Enclosure Act. Ichabod

The Grosvenor Hotel itself is much the same today, although the grounds are different. The large red-brick building was north of the market place.

Another view of the market place. Most of the houses and shops were built when the village was started.

The houses and shops on Hucknall Road were demolished as part of the Carrington clearance area.

built the handsome mansion known as Mapperley Hall on the other side of Mansfield Road.

When Wright sold off the building plots he called the new settlement Carrington because he was a friend of Robert Smith, who had been created a peer and took the title Lord Carrington. There had been a former Lord Carrington who had also been a Smith, and the peerage had lapsed when he died. Robert Smith had used his banking and financial expertise to help the government of William Pitt the Younger, who helped Smith to obtain his peerage. This was commemorated by a wit who wrote 'Pitt took the pen from behind Smith's ear and made him a peer.'

The newly created Carrington followed the pattern set by New Basford about the same time in forming an industrial village taking advantage of the growth of the textile trade when Heathcote's patent for a lace machine expired. A deed drawn up in July 1827 referred to 25 tenements recently erected. The names of 18 tenants were given, while the remainder were built but still untenanted. *White's Directory* of 1832 describes Carrington as another new village, consisting partly of handsome villas, occupied by merchants and lace manufacturers who had their warehouses in Nottingham. The latter are shown on a map as being in semi-detached pairs on the Mansfield Road. The directory gives the names and occupations of some of the residents. They included John Hopkins, lace

manufacturer, John Rogers, hosier, William Russell, lace thread manufacturer and William Taylor, bobbin and carriage maker. Besides bakers, butchers and other shopkeepers, there was the King William IV public house and three beer houses. The largest category of occupations was bobbin net makers, of which there were 32.

In 1867, William Felkin published his *A History of the Machine-Wrought Hosiery and Lace Manufactures*. He was able to explain the development of the bobbin net lace industry, as he had worked for John Heathcote, who took out a patent for making true lace on a machine adapted from the stocking frame. Although many had tried to do this without complete success it was not until 1808 that Heathcote took out his patent. Felkin states that this was not solely the work of Heathcote himself but was the culmination of the efforts of many other inventors. The problem had been to imitate on a machine the making of lace by hand, using the traditional pillow method. Heathcote perfected the machine process using a system of moving bobbins, hence the name bobbin net lace. Other products could be made by other arrangements of bobbins, but these did not produce true lace.

When Heathcote's patent expired in 1825, those who had enough money could acquire a bobbin net machine. A further advancement is mentioned by

The designer of these Edwardian houses had the foresight to provide room for wheelie bins.

Felkin, who describes the work of Thomas Robert Sewell, who started a factory at Carrington with circular power-driven machines. He was a remarkable man, born in around 1788 near Nottingham who, although he had only a rudimentary education, acquired a good knowledge of science and also of the working of the stocking frame. He made improvements to the frame and drew his own patterns.

From its early planned development, Carrington started to develop beyond its original boundaries mainly northwards towards Sherwood, which had been founded at about the same time and was growing in a southerly direction. This was recognised in 1843 when a new Anglican church, St John Evangelist, was erected on Mansfield Road through the generosity of Ichabod Wright. In 1877 a new publisher in the directory business for Nottingham, Morris and Company, published a directory and gazeetter. This has separate sections for each of the districts, as well as the borough, and is interesting in that it is the last such directory before the suburbs, including Carrington, became incorporated into the borough. It gave the population in 1871 as 2,543 and added that the Wesleyans and Baptists had places of worship there, as well as National Schools. It listed the names of 20 clergy, gentry and private residents and gave

another list of trades and professions. The streets named are practically the same as those shown in the 1827 auction notice, but it is a sign of the development that had already taken place that there were various people listed as living in the Market Place. These are mainly shops – a butcher, bootmaker and other shopkeepers, including Lenton Co-operative Stores (Miss Alice Hyde, manageress). There is no mention of bobbin net or lace makers, as by this time they had been absorbed into the new factories. Robert Burton had one, as a lace manufacturer, and William Mills was a manufacturer of muslin goods. Carrington Brewery Company, King William IV, the White Hart, the New Inn and the Grosvenor Hotel also made sure the inhabitants did not die of thirst.

Recently demolished to make way for the Clarendon College site, the newsagent's shop was formerly the entrance to Carrington LNER station.

The mention of the Grosvenor Hotel, Mansfield Road, indicates that some development had started to take place south of the junction with Hucknall Road. John Harrison Williamson, the licensee, was also described as a horse dealer. Both he and his son sometimes rode as jockeys on the nearby racecourse, and John become famous for winning the Grand National.

In view of the recent foundation of Carrington and its nearness to the borough, the extension of the latter made little difference to the district. It continued to expand in the last quarter of the 19th

Carrington Lido has gone but its site, with a children's playground, is a small oasis off Mansfield Road.

century, benefiting from the general increase in prosperity of the enlarged borough, not only from the booming lace trade, but also from the increasing diversity of newer industries.

The start of the 20th century saw two major developments in transport that affected Carrington. Already the railway line of the new Great Central Company had come through Carrington, with a station at the end of Gregory Boulevard. The line from there went through a tunnel to Victoria Station, opened to passenger traffic in 1901. At about the same time, the first electric trams started to run from Nottingham along Mansfield Road to Carrington and Sherwood, every five minutes from 7.15am to 11.15pm. Most of the old street names had changed and new streets had been built – Jenner Street, Knox Street, Wesley Street and Birchin Street. Eighteen commercial establishments were listed in *Wright's Directory* of 1902 under Market Place. These included Hozene Company, Portable Furnace and Patents Company and a

branch of Lady Bay Laundry. Carrington by this time was more or less built-up and there was no visible difference between its boundary and that of Sherwood.

The 1920s and 1930s saw little further change in Carrington except for those common to the rest of the city, such as increasing numbers of cars, the cessation of the trams and their replacement by buses and trolley buses. The 1930s did however see two developments in leisure facilities, the Curzon

The splendid classical façade of Thomas Forman's building remains, although the printing firm has gone.

Cinema and the open-air swimming pool, both on Mansfield Road near to each other.

After World War Two, Carrington was one of the earliest areas to be declared a clearance area, leading to the demolition of all the original houses, which were then 130 years old. New shops with flats above were erected on part of the site, and a new school with its own playing field forms an open space on Hucknall Road. A limited number of properties on Hucknall Road were demolished later, as was the Curzon Cinema, which could not compete with television. Similarly Carrington Lido could not compare with sunny Spain and it was closed. Its site has been made into a pleasant green oasis between Mansfield Road and Loscoe Road. The railway station disappeared when the line from the north to Victoria Station was closed.

The triangle between Sherwood Rise and Mansfield Road has been redeveloped, mainly by the Clarendon College, with a small rest garden. Apart from these recent alterations Carrington is now a quiet mainly residential area with mostly Victorian and Edwardian houses, but with some small pockets of 20th-century dwellings.

CLIFTON

In 1906 the Revd Rosslyn Bruce, the rector of Clifton, published *The Clifton Book*. In the introduction he stated that 'a book about Clifton to be characteristic should smell of the fresh-ploughed soil and resound with the song of thrushes'. In the Domesday Book, William Peverel was described as having two ploughs and the freemen, villages and smallholders had nine ploughs. Ulfkell also had one bovate of land, with one villager with two ploughing oxen. Ploughing had been a feature of Clifton for at least 900 years. Fifty years after Bruce wrote the song of thrushes could still be heard, although there was little ploughing done.

From its name it is clear that Clifton was an

The original volume of Dr Thoroton's *Antiquities* included this engraving of Clifton House, as the Hall was then known.

Anglo-Saxon settlement, a tun means a farm, in this case standing on a cliff above the River Trent. In 1086, when the Domesday Book recorded the number of men as 31, it was larger in population than many other villages. It was also more important, having a priest and a church, a mill and 12 acres of meadow. William Peverel also had 'soc' in a number of other villages, which meant that they were subject to his jurisdiction and they had to pay fines or acknowledgements to him. One of these villages was Wilford, which adjoined Clifton, and later owners of land at Clifton also owned land at Wilford.

Was this Clifton's first taxi service?

There was a man named Sir Alvered de Clifton who was guardian of Nottingham Castle under William Peverel, but although he had taken his surname from the village, he was not the owner of the land or lord of the manor. Until the 13th century the lordship was held by a family named de Rodes, who sold the manors of Clifton and Wilford to Sir Gervase de Clifton. This family still held the lands in 1906 and were to do so until 1950 when the last owner sold Clifton to the Nottingham Corporation.

The centre of the old village has the LTI cottage in the centre.

Dr Robert Thoroton wrote his book *The Antiquities of Nottinghamshire* in 1676 and was able to trace the Clifton family's descent from Sir Alvered down to his time through an unbroken line of males. He did this for most of the other landed families of the county but his account of the Clifton family is more detailed than most of the others. This was because he was a doctor of medicine and one of his patients was Sir Gervase Clifton, the first baronet, who became known as the gentle Sir Gervase. Most of the male Cliftons were named Gervase or Robert and many of them became knights or baronets.

Thoroton's Gervase is described by him as 'certainly more gentle than his grandfather being generally the most noted person for his courtesy, he was very prosperous and beloved of all'. He went on to describe Sir Gervase's death in 1666 saying 'he received from me the certain notice of his near approaching death'. He added that both his ureters were so petrified that no urine could descend into his bladder. Dr Thoroton appears to have carried out or witnessed a post-mortem examination of the body, which he tells us showed that one of the kidneys had been 'totally stopped with a wonderful great stone'.

His book also contains a description of the tombs in the church of St Mary, which adjoins Clifton Hall, the residence of the family, and illustrations of some of them. In 1790 John Throsby produced a new edition of Thoroton's work and added some notes of his own. He did this for Clifton and mentioned some of the tombs erected after Thoroton's time. Of one of these he writes 'Joseph commonly called the Black Prince, a negro, who was converted to the Christian faith in 1685, is also remembered here. It appears he was brought up in the Clifton family and grew to nearly the height of seven feet. His height is marked in the church porch.'

Sir Gervase was married seven times and when he died his son, also Sir Gervase, succeeded his father as the second baronet. He did not inherit the estate as his wild disposition led to his being described by his father as his greatest sorrow because of his way of life. The estate went to a son by Sir Gervase's second wife, Sir Clifford Clifton. His son Sir William became the third baronet but when he died unmarried the baronetcy and estates went to another Sir Gervase, the grandson of his sixth wife. He had 15 sons and one daughter and he and the succeeding fifth to eighth baronets lived in the house for the next 160 years. They continued to live at Clifton as country squires managing the estates. They established the village as a 'closed' one, that is one where they ensured that no one came to live in it from outside in case they became a burden on the rates. The effect of this was to keep Clifton as a small village until the middle of the 20th century. The rector in his book referred to Mr James Moss, who he said was grandfather to about half the parish. This is confirmed by the 1891 census when there were four families of that name there. They were outnumbered by the Reckless families of whom there were five, while there were also four Butler families. This was in a parish of 360 people.

When the eighth Baronet, Sir Juckes Clifton, died in 1852, he was succeeded by his son Sir Robert Clifton who became MP for Nottingham in 1861. Revd Rosslyn Bruce gives a short history of his character as MP and wrote: 'A strange sort of popular epidemic of loyal and devoted adherence seems to have caught hold of Nottingham, and raised the jolly rollicking open-handed and frank young squire into little short of an idol'.

Hardy Cottage, also thatched, is another of Clifton's listed buildings.

In *The Thoroton Society Transactions for 1953* Professor A.C. Wood wrote at greater length about Sir Robert. He was rather less generous than the rector, giving more details of Sir Robert's early life. He was born when his father was 57 years old and he was over-indulged as a child, with no discipline and too much to spend. He frittered away his time and fell in with the sporting fraternity, owning racehorses from the age of 19. He soon fell into debt and was obliged to live in Paris for many years. When he returned to England he seems to have spent his first nine years as lord of the manor and squire like his forbears. He was, however, a completely different character, which endeared him to the working-class men of Nottingham. His frank

and open nature made him at home with them, along with his generosity and complete lack of the reserve with which the gentry usually treated the working classes. It was this as much as anything which helped him to be elected as an independent MP for Nottingham. Professor Wood describes in detail how this came about through the political machinations that accompanied Parliamentary elections. Nottingham elections at this time were notorious for their bribery and mob violence.

The village was formerly known as Clifton-cum-Glapton and this was one of its thatched cottages, which has been demolished.

Sir Robert was elected in 1861 and again in 1865 but his election was declared invalid due to the bribery carried out by his supporters, although this was not of his doing. He was elected again in 1868 but died in May the next year from typhoid fever, aged 43. He was unmarried, so the baronetcy lapsed and the Clifton estate passed to a cousin, Henry Markham. When he died in 1896, the estate went to the son of Sir Robert's sister, who had married Sir Harvey Bruce. He was Colonel Harvey Bruce and was succeeded by his grandson Percy Robert Bruce, who changed his surname to Clifton. His son Lieutenant Colonel Peter Clifton became the last owner of the estate until it was sold to Nottingham Corporation in 1950.

The Revd Rosslyn Bruce who became the rector was a nephew of Sir Harvey Bruce. His book gives a number of fascinating glimpses of life at Clifton in

Holly Lodge, a pseudo-classical house near the Hall, has been demolished and a new house built on the site.

Clifton Grove, photographed in 1939, long before Dutch elm disease ravaged it.

the 19th century and in earlier years. He mentions a local tradition that said that when an aumbry, a small square space, was made in the church wall, the bones of two unborn babies were found and said to be three or four hundred years old. This gave rise to what he describes as 'curious and interesting suggestions'. Unfortunately he gives no details of these!

He also refers to a Mr William Spencer, who died aged 76 in 1871. He was an antiquarian and student of local lore, schoolmaster, farmer, doctor, dentist, parish constable, overseer, rate collector and ferret breeder to the parish. Another anecdote

he relates refers to the 'considerable industry' of most of the cottages in the summer months in providing teas for visitors. One such old lady kept a Visitors' Book in which she was proud to have the signatures of Sir Henry Irving and Miss Ellen Terry.

His book contains a 'Who's Who in 1906' which gives a list of 77 persons who between them held 125 offices. These include the lord of the manor and the rector, as well as the parish clerk, church cleaner, pasture master, post-master, parish constable, school managers, footballers and cricketers, teachers of day, night and Sunday school, lending library committees, district nurse, choir bell-ringers and organ blower. Mrs Bruce conducted the mother's meeting, clothing club and savings bank. All this without a public house, which the lords of the manor would not allow, shows what a self-contained community Clifton was then.

The first half of the 20th century saw Clifton largely unchanged, the single ownership being able to resist some of the changes affecting much of England. The second half of the century, however, did bring changes, which few people could have foreseen. As early as 1943, Nottingham City Council was looking for land outside the city boundary for housing purposes. After a long and at times acrimonious process of negotiation, particularly with Colonel Clifton and Notting-hamshire County Council, the city acquired the whole of the Clifton estate. From 1 April 1952 it became part of the City of Nottingham, although the first council houses had already been built on the land east of the road leading to Wilford. These were the first of some 7,000 houses which were built in the ensuing years, making it one of the largest council estates in the country. The tenants were all from the City Council's housing waiting list for people who did not have a separate home of their own. Access to the waiting list was limited to people in lower income groups. As a result the earliest tenants were mainly younger families with husbands working in nearby Nottingham. As the estate was completely separated from the rest of the city, there were few facilities available at first. The bus service to Nottingham went through Wilford and West Bridgford, as there was no suitable bridge over the river apart from Trent Bridge. The estate became known for the efforts of some of the earlier tenants to seek accommodation in the city by way of exchanges. Advertisements often appeared fastened to a tree at the entrance to the estate, which became known as the 'tree of knowledge'.

Additional facilities in the shape of shops, schools, libraries, churches and recreation grounds were gradually provided and a new bridge over the River Trent was also built to give a more direct route to the city. In time residents grew to appreciate the clean air, as coal fires were not allowed, and the nearness to the countryside. This is reflected by the fact that when tenants were allowed to buy their own houses, Clifton had the highest percentage take-up of all the city's estates.

The City Council agreed to preserve the village as far as possible and it was later made a conservation area. Some newer dwellings have been built but have not altered the character of the village. Colonel Clifton left the Hall, which became Clifton Grammar School for Girls for a time and then became part of Trent Polytechnic for teacher training. A new campus north of the village was built for the Polytechnic, now Nottingham Trent University. Other land on the west side of the estate has been developed as far as Clifton Grove. This path, lined each on side with elm trees, was planted in 1690 by the then squire of Clifton. Sadly its

beauty suffered the ravages of Dutch elm disease and is now not as attractive as it was when Henry Kirke White, a young poet from Nottingham, wrote his poem of 500 lines entitled *Clifton Grove*, where: 'Here lonely wandering o'er the Sylvan Bower/I came to pass the meditative hour.'

He also used the poem to relate the legendary story of the Fair Maid of Clifton. She was Margaret, who lived there during the Wars of the Roses. She promised to wait for Bateman, who had to spend three years abroad. On his return he found that she had been married six months earlier, whereupon he drowned himself in the Trent at dead of night. After her child was born, Margaret did likewise in 'her own and murdered lover's mutual grave'.

The Trent also figures in another of Clifton's legends. It was said that when a death was about to occur in the Clifton family a sturgeon would be seen swimming in the river below the village.

Today Clifton village remains a picturesque scene, with its green and dovecote, old village school, thatched cottages, church and Hall. The latter is at present unoccupied and the plan is to demolish some of the more recent additions and convert the Hall into flats. The residents of the dwellings on both sides of the former country lane are also facing change with some concern. The A453 road, a main approach to the M1 and Ratcliffe-on-Soar generating station, is insufficient for the volume of traffic. After years of discussion and argument a decision has been made in principle to widen the road to a dual carriageway.

FOREST FIELDS

Salmon's map of 1861 shows the borough's northern boundary with Lenton to be what today is Gregory Boulevard. Within the borough was the Forest, with its cricket ground and racecourse. On

the Lenton side there was shown a small part containing six quite large houses, in an area marked as being in Radford parish. The houses were at the end of Basford Road, now Sherwood Rise, and the

An elaborate date stone, 1881, on one of the earliest houses to be built in Forest Fields.

houses are still there today, on First Avenue. Sanderson's map of 1835 shows that another part of Lenton, Hyson Green, was also built up and this too was in Radford parish. Between these two the land was still open country northwards as far as the boundary with Basford, which at that date was built up as New Basford, with Elm Avenue as its most southerly street.

After 1877 these boundaries were irrelevant as far as administration was concerned, as the borough was extended, taking in Lenton, Radford and Basford. The latter remained as ecclesiastical parishes until they were divided into new ones as new churches were built.

Tarbotton's map of 1877 was drawn up to give the first map with details such as street names for all the adjoining parishes, which were to be brought into the borough. This shows that Hyson Green was still covering the same area as earlier, while on Sherwood Rise, Second, Third and Fourth Avenues

Foxhall Lodge is an imposing house, as befitted the first owner, Stanley Birkin, son of Sir Thomas Isaac.

A former factory on Gladstone Street has been converted into flats. The balconies are new.

had been built on. The proposed new road was completed in 1880 and named Gregory Boulevard. This paved the way for the land to the north to be developed. Since 1874 all proposals for building properties in the borough had to be submitted to the Nottingham Corporation for approval. Where such proposals involved constructing new streets, a plan of them had to be submitted as well, and the developer was expected to give the new streets a name. In June 1883 the first scheme for the land north of the new boulevard was submitted to the Corporation and approved. The plan showed that the site covered about 50 acres, with a frontage on Gregory Boulevard of about a quarter-mile. The street on the northern edge was Gladstone Street and those running north to south were named as Burford Road, Russell Road, Stanley Road, Harcourt Road and Leslie Road. The plan also showed that the lands to the east and west of the site were owned by Nottingham Real Estate Investment Company. The area between Leslie Road and Sherwood Rise was to be developed later.

The scheme was named the Forest Ville Estate but this name had been given earlier to the small area described above on which First Avenue was built, so later the whole area became known as Forest Fields. This gave a clearly defined suburb of about 100 acres.

The 1883 scheme had been submitted by Thomas Isaac Birkin, then of Ruddington Grange. He was the son of Richard Birkin, who had built up a lace manufacturer's business as described in the chapter on New Basford. His son developed the business after his father's death to an even greater

Second Avenue is one of the four numbered avenues on the west side of Sherwood Rise.

An individually designed house at the corner of Wiverton Road and Sherwood Rise has a modern sign on the left. It was designed by Watson Fothergill.

The Norris almshouses on Berridge Road, erected in 1893, were also designed by Watson Fothergill and show some of his typical features, especially the chimneys.

extent, later being created a baronet with descendants who have become famous in other ways. Thomas already had a large factory on the other side of Gladstone Street, as well as others including the T.C. Hine-designed business in Broadway in the Lace Market.

Birkin had purchased the land from the Trustees of the Gregory Estate and it was subject to a number of covenants as to the type and quality of the houses to be built and the prohibition of any industrial buildings. Birkin had presumably purchased the land as an investment and he did not develop the estate himself. Instead he divided the site into 209 separate plots which were sold to builders and developers. This resulted in a variety of types of houses ranging from detached and semi-detached villas to terraces without forecourts. The development can be traced by reference to the deposited plans, as all those up to 1948 are held by Nottinghamshire Archives. The Corporation appears to have adopted a policy of only approving plans which maintained the general character of the area. This was no doubt done to prevent the building of houses that were no better than the many thousands of older houses in the town. Its success can be measured by the fact that all the houses are still there, apart from one recent

exception. This is at the Gregory Boulevard end of Burford Road, where the large houses between it and Noel Street have been demolished.

There must have soon been a sufficient number of houses with children as in 1889 an infants' school was opened on Stanley Road. High Pavement School was opened in a new building adjoining the infants' school, but this was for the transfer of pupils from the old school on the street of the same name in the Lace Market. *Wright's Directory* for 1889 lists 86 houses on Burford Road, although it was not completed then. The occupiers are all either middle class, owners of businesses, three school-masters, cashiers, solicitors' clerks, cigar merchant; or skilled workers such as draughtsmen and designers. The curator at the Natural History Museum lived there as did an inspector of schools, W.J. Abel. A few years later he became the clerk to Nottingham School Board.

By the beginning of the 20th century there were 120 houses on Burford Road and 74 on Foxhall Road, which was not fully developed. A number of streets such as Bradgate Road, Ewart Road, Windermere Road and Austen Avenue were not yet

The temple on Berridge Road was formerly the Apollo Cinema, previously known as the Berridge.

The school on Gregory Boulevard, built as a grammar school for girls, was changed to the Forest School and is awaiting demolition.

constructed. The period up to 1914 saw a large number of new houses built in all suburbs of the city, and by 1914 Forest Fields was more or less completely built on. Bradgate Road was built in around 1909, with Forest Fields Council schools as well. Some of the building schemes were quite large, including one of 49 houses on Stanley Road.

The period from 1919 to 1939 saw one or two notable changes. In 1931 the undeveloped land between Burford Road and Leslie Road was used to build the Manning School for Girls, leaving High Pavement School as a boys school. The Berridge Road picture house was built just in time for the 'talkies' era, later simplifying its name to the Apollo.

By 1939, some of the changes in the area reflected the social changes of the post-1918 era, especially the large houses on Gregory Boulevard. This included the use of one as a hotel, while another became Ellerslie House hospital and two adjoining houses became Health Department Clinics.

Apart from Gregory Boulevard, where none of the buildings are private houses, the general appearance of this residential suburb has hardly changed. The Apollo Cinema is now a temple, reflecting the social change of the inner city as a whole and the increased occupancy by the ethnic minorities who have taken up residence in the last 30 or 40 years.

HYSON GREEN

In 1799 the Lenton and Radford Enclosure award granted one and a quarter acres of land to William Bingham. This was part of the land that extended from today's Gregory Boulevard to the New Basford boundary. The abstract of title to 3 Pleasant Row, the dwelling which was later built on

this plot, goes back to an indenture showing that William Bingham, maltster of Radford, and Sarah his wife disposed of the land on 17 May 1804.

The house was probably built in the 1820s as part of a row of similar houses in a small part of Radford parish, which was surrounded by Lenton parish. Sanderson's Map of 1835 shows this row, on the west side of the road to Basford, together with a larger area on the east side and another one to the south of Pleasant Row, all with the name Hyson Green.

A notice of an auction in 1846 of three houses on Pleasant Row, numbers 34, 43 and 44, described them as well-built and convenient dwelling houses in Ison Green with a yard, outbuildings and garden. The notice also stated that they carried the right to a freehold vote for the north division of Nottinghamshire. This was in accordance with the Reform Act of 1832, which gave owners of freehold property above a certain value the right to vote in elections for knights of the shire, i.e. county MPs. The Pleasant Row houses were said to have been erected as a co-operative housing scheme, or club. Similar schemes elsewhere had the name Club Row. Later, larger scale maps show that the Pleasant Row houses had 100ft gardens.

The name Hyson Green was spelled as Ison Green on occasions – presumably a corruption of Hyson. The reason for the name of Hyson is said to be 'from the tea gardens to which parties frequently walked in summer to quench their thirst with hyson and other nectarous draughts for which purpose one of these establishments is still in existence'. This was given in *White's Directory* for 1832, which describes Hyson Green as another well-built village which had been erected in the last 10 years. It was in Radford parish, although most of the land around was in Lenton parish. This was a situation that had arisen in the days when Lenton Priory was founded and William Peverel granted it lands in many other places from which the Priory received income.

White's Directory goes on to say that the village had a population of about 2,000 souls and it mentions the names of the principal streets, some of which survived until the 1960s. It also listed four nonconformist chapels. There was no Anglican church until 1844 when St Paul's was built as a chapelry on Pleasant Row opposite the houses. The directory gave a list of the occupations of the people of Radford, of whom 250 were bobbin net makers, and 50 of them were in Hyson Green. The population of the district grew slowly, and was said to be 2,300 in 1853. However, it was to start expanding after Radford and Lenton came into the borough in 1877. It benefitted, as Lenton and Radford did, from the making of Gregory Boulevard and the creation of a new continuous road from Alfreton Road to Basford and Bulwell.

By the beginning of the 20th century the boundaries of Hyson Green had been extended into Radford and it is rather a matter of opinion where one ends and the other begins. The planned formation of Forest Fields towards the east meant that Noel Street formed a border on that side. On the west the growth as far as Alfreton Road was accompanied by a similar growth towards Hyson Green from Bobbers Mill Road, which could be regarded as part of the former.

A view of the rear of houses on Saville Street in 1958, with some of the houses have sliding sash windows to give more light for the stocking frame.

Bevel Street was a narrow passageway leading from Gregory Boulevard to Forest Street, now part of the site of Braidwood Court.

The last two decades of the 19th century not only saw a great increase in the number of houses but also of other buildings, which expanded the sense of unity of the district. One of those was a new church, St Stephen's on Bobbers Mill Road, which was built in 1898. This had been preceded by an iron mission church on a temporary basis in 1883 near the site of the permanent church. There was already a St Stephen's church in Nottingham, on Bunkers Hill. This was demolished as part of the redevelopment of that area to form the Victoria Station and the Great Central Railway and the title was transferred to the Bobbers Mill Road church, along with many artefacts.

No.34 Lenton Street in 1960, the home of the Little Company of Mary from 1877, was built on the site of the demolished convent. It was started by Mary Potter who founded a community of nursing nuns who used the building until a new Mary Potter Health Centre was built nearby.

A directory of 1902 shows that half a mile of Radford Road from Bentinck Road was, on both sides, occupied by commercial properties, mainly shops selling all kinds of wares – food, clothing, as well as pawnbrokers, watch-makers, a piano warehouse, china and glass dealers, florist and seedsmen, and even a horse keeper. There were a number of public houses, as well as a dancing academy and the Grand Theatre. Leading off Radford Road on both sides were 32 streets, mainly lined with houses, but also including small industrial premises such as cycle makers, perambulator manufacturers, french polishers and a muslin manufacturer. The only large industries were a brass-founders and, on Forest Street, Abbot's

factory with 13 tenants. The adjoining street, Lenton Street, had Hyson Green's most surprising building, the Convent of Maternal Heart. At the junction of Radford Road and Gregory Boulevard was a police station, mortuary, library and Methodist church.

The Grand Theatre on Radford Road alternated as a theatre and an early cinema until it became solely a cinema.

The first 60 years of the 20th century saw Hyson Green change, much like other inner suburbs of Nottingham – trams, trolley buses, buses, motor traffic, cinemas and new retailers all moved in. It was to experience a similar need to deal with the ageing and deteriorating early houses by clearance schemes. Two or three schemes affecting small areas came in 1958, while a much larger scheme involved practically all the dwellings between Gregory

The Leno's Cinema on Radford Road was one of Hyson Green's earliest 'cinematographic theatres' as they were called originally. It is now used as a furniture dealers but is up for sale. The road in this photograph was closed on one side while the new tram track was being laid.

A St Paul's school group taken in 1910, showing Miss Bertha Marshall's class with the headmaster.

Just opposite Leno's, at the corner of Bobbers Mill Road, is the Old General public house with its unusual sign. This is an effigy of Benjamin Mayo, an early 19th-century Nottingham man with a military pseudonym.

Braidwood Court, a high-rise block of flats, was the only part of the redevelopment of Hyson Green in the 1970s which survived the subsequent demolitions.

Boulevard and Berridge Road to the east of Radford Road. The redevelopment as low-rise deck-access flats and maisonettes proved to be so unpopular that, as at Old Basford and Balloon Wood, the whole scheme was demolished, being replaced by more traditional houses and a supermarket. The 15-storey high Braidwood Court did escape the defects which affected the rest of the scheme, and it survives.

Hyson Green, and particularly Radford Road with its preponderance of retail shops, suffered from changed shopping habits and other social changes in the 20th century. Efforts have been made to bring new life to the area, with some financial assistance and co-operation with local residents. The past two years have seen the residents and traders faced with new problems from the construction of the modern tram system, which is due to start operating at the end of 2003.

This should bring relief to Hyson Green.

LENTON

Lenton is another of the four Anglo-Saxon settlements that took their names from the otherwise undistinguished River Leen, its name meaning simply 'Leen town'. It was about a mile due south of its neighbour Radford. When parish boundaries were defined, Lenton became much larger in extent than Radford.

In the Domesday Book Lenton has two entries, but it is relatively small with land for four and a half ploughs and 10 freemen, villagers and small-holders. There is no evidence that life in Lenton was any different than in Radford for 40 years after the Normans came.

In 1103, however, an event occurred which was to make a profound difference to the two parishes. This was the founding of a Cluniac house, Lenton Priory, by William Peverel, the constable of Nottingham Castle. As the natural son of William, the Norman king of England from 1066, he was possessed of many holdings of land in Nottinghamshire and other counties and so was able to endow the Priory with properties. These enabled the priory to become one of the wealthiest and most powerful religious houses in the county. It even had the patronage of the borough of Nottingham's three parishes. It was granted its own fair, which on occasion was to be a source of friction with the borough, which had its own fair, both being for trade.

Some of the lands which were appropriated for the priory were in the neighbouring parish of Radford and this later caused no little confusion in ascertaining which was Lenton parish and which Radford. An even more anomalous situation arose at Bestwood (then known as Beskwood). King Henry I granted the monks the right to have carts of dead wood and heath from his royal park there. This seems to have led to the assumption that Bestwood Park was

The houses on the left side of the photograph were on Gregory Street with Churchill Street and Old Church Street leading off. The photograph was taken in 1959 prior to the demolition of the houses.

part of Lenton parish until the Borough Extension Act of 1877.

Lenton Priory was one of the early victims of the dissolution of the monasteries and its destruction was carried out in dramatic fashion. In 1538 the priory, along with seven monks and a priest, was found guilty of treason and three of the men were executed. The priory was dissolved by forfeiture without compensation. This enabled the Crown to order the demolition of the prior's buildings, some of the stone being used to make a roadway beneath which the ruins still remain. The lands were sold off, with William Gregory acquiring the manor of Lenton in 1630. His heirs remained the owners of most of the land of Lenton until the 20th century. He was an alderman of the borough and one of his descendants married a member of another leading Nottingham family, the Sherwins. This eventually led to the estate becoming the Sherwin-Gregory estate. Both names are perpetuated by streets in Lenton.

The Sherwood Forest survey of 1609 treats Lenton and Radford jointly, with a combined map. The various closes and holdings are described in 37 sections, most of them being occupied by different tenants. Two parts are described as common to Lenton and Radford. The map shows the position of the 'towns' where the dwellings were, there being considerably more in Lenton than in Radford. The Protestation Return of 1641/2 had no difficulty in having separate lists for both parishes, Lenton with 147 names having twice as many as Radford. A similar distinction is shown in the Hearth Tax Return of 1674 – Lenton had four large houses with nine hearths or more, although the largest is 21 for Lord Willoughby of 'Bescolike', no doubt an interpretation of Bestwood, the detached part of Lenton. Very few of the names in the Protestation Return of 1641/2 appear in the Hearth Tax Return.

Dr Robert Thoroton heads his account of Lenton by adding Morton and Knighton, but he explains that the latter two are both 'lost'. He deals mainly with the many places in England which were sources of income to Lenton Priory. He goes on to name several citizens of London who were appointed by King Henry VIII to form a commission to dispose of the lands of the priory.

This picture postcard shows the view of Gregory Street looking the opposite way to the bottom picture.

This drawing by Thomas Hammond shows the rear of the White Hart Inn on Gregory Street. The garden had an entrance to the debtors' prison, which was part of the inn for some time.

Lenton appears to have had a rather unusual vicar in the 17th century. A note in the Protestation Return refers to Robert Ollerenshaw, vicar, by noting that 'On 13 July 1629 an indictment was against (him) of Lenton, clerk, for being a "night walker" and he was indicted also in 1635 for occupying a temporal [i.e. not glebe] farm.' A Commonwealth commission in 1650 described him as a 'preaching minister at present but is a drunkard and of an ill conversation.'

In 1743, the return to Archbishop Herring gave the number of families as 84, with three Presbyterians, one Baptist and three Quakers. The vicar, George Wayte, added that he did not live in the parish and he had a dispensation because he was the under-master of the Free School in Nottingham.

An Act of 1758–9 set up a turnpike road from Chapel Bar, Nottingham, to Derby, which passed through Lenton. In 1795 the Nottingham Canal was completed, part of which ran through Lenton, more or less parallel to the River Leen. A year later it was reported that a boat had passed along the Beeston Cut. This joined the Nottingham Canal near the Nottingham border and met the River Trent at Beeston, passing through the southern part of Lenton. The cut had been made because of the difficulty boats had at the ancient, many-arched Trent Bridge. It also enabled a connection with the larger canal network westwards. Beeston Canal remains navigable today and appears as a continuation of the Nottingham Canal, which has been filled in to the west.

By the time of the Census in 1801 Lenton's population had risen to 893, but had been overtaken in numbers by Radford at 2,269. For the rest of the 19th century Lenton lagged behind Radford in population, despite its greater acreage. Nevertheless, *White's Directory* of 1832 was able to

Taken in 1964, this picture shows Gregory Street to the west of the White Hart Inn.

No.3 Gregory Street is known as the old Manor House, the real one having been demolished. The windows are a striking feature of the house.

report that Lenton had 'felt the manufacturing impulse of Nottingham' and had a population of 3,077, in 631 houses, 400 of which had been built in the previous 10 years. It had started, as at Basford and Radford, by forming new villages, Middleton Place and Spring Close. It described Middleton Place as a new village, a quarter of a mile north-east of the old village with more than 200 houses, all built within the last 10 years. It added that it is commonly known as New Lenton, and is marked as such on Sanderson's map of 1835. *White's Directory* also refers to Lenton as a large and beautiful village 'consisting principally of handsome villas and neat cottages with gardens and shrubberies some of them stuccoed in the gothic style'. It also names several handsome mansions west of the village, five of them with names prefixed by Lenton, as well as High Fields house. These all still exist, all but one being part of the University of Nottingham campus.

The parish church in Old Lenton was a small one, built after the dissolution of the priory and incorporating part of a monastic building. The move of people and industry to New Lenton prompted the building in 1842 of Holy Trinity Church there.

At the first census after Lenton became part of the borough its population of 10,194 was still lower than the figure for Radford in 1851. The population was concentrated in more or less

separate districts. Old Lenton was the area around Abbey Street and Gregory Street, with a smaller section called Spring Close. New Lenton was described in directories as Lenton Sands, around Willoughby Street. Most of the remainder of the district was open country as far as the boundary with Beeston stretching southwards as far as the River Trent.

The Butt houses on Derby Road were demolished 40 years ago. The name may have signified the use of the land behind for archery practice.

One of the largest industrial enterprises was Thomas Bayley's leather works. The building on Leen Gate has now been converted into living accommodation. The lace industry was confined to the Willoughby Street area, with a tenement factory, Walker's, on Preston Street and Willoughby Street. The first major effect of the borough extension was the building of the four boulevards forming three sides of a square. The southern section started at the end of Canal Street and extended as far as Church Street. The first part of this section was later renamed Castle Boulevard. By 1887, a Board School and some houses had been built near Osmaston Street. By 1902 a number of new streets had been built on the west side of the boulevard, including Faraday Road on which the Raleigh Cycle works were built in 1897, the business having been so named from its original location on the street of that name off Alfreton Road.

The years between 1900 and 1914 saw a considerable increase in the number of new houses built. An application for approval in 1901 by the Pearson-Gregory estate was for 200 houses between Ilkeston and Derby Road, on Rothesay Avenue, Kimbolton Avenue and Ashburnham Avenue. By 1914 the whole of the triangle formed by Lenton Boulevard, Ilkeston Road and Derby Road had been completely built up. On the opposite side of Derby Road, Rolleston Drive and Harrington Drive formed an extension of the adjoining industrial Willoughby Street area, but without industry and consisting of better quality housing. The west-side of Lenton Boulevard had new streets running westwards but with an open space in the centre.

The old village remained largely unaltered but there was movement on the west side towards the district of Dunkirk. The name first appears in an Ordnance Survey map of about 1825. It remained more or less a route to Nottingham Canal until development started in around 1885 when a small estate grew up. This consisted of several streets on

each side of what by 1914 was called Beeston Road as far as Greenfield Street.

Beyond Greenfield Street was open country as far as the Beeston boundary. In 1920 the City Council applied for an extension of its boundary to include Beeston itself. At a public enquiry, the counsel for Beeston described Lenton in somewhat highly coloured language. His intention was to show that it formed a green belt between the two areas and therefore should not become part of the industrialised city. It was he said, fair hunting country, with all the characteristics of an English countryside – hedgerows, fields, cattle grazing and parks attached to country houses.

Shortly after this Lenton was to see the start of changes that were to continue for the rest of the 20th century. At the end of 1919 Sir Jesse Boot (later Baron Trent) made the first purchase of land at Lenton which led to his acquiring the estate as far as the Beeston boundary. Although he had intended

The pavilion at the end of the lake at Highfields has been demolished and a new arts centre erected on the site.

to use it for industrial purposes, he instead gave it to Nottingham Corporation. Part of it was to be the site of the University College and part for the establishment of a park. This resulted in the building of new premises for the college, the establishment of a park, with a boating lake and pavilion and sports grounds, together with an open-air swimming pool, Highfields Lido. Most of the former mansions were used by the college as residences for students and staff and other ancillary purposes. The whole scheme also involved the creation of a new wide road to Beeston, University Boulevard. Lenton was also affected, along with Wollaton, by the start of the outer ring road, Middleton Boulevard.

In this period Old Lenton saw the building of a large block of flats by Boots Company on Penn Avenue and memorial homes by Sir Albert Ball in memory of his son, Captain Albert Ball VC, the World War One fighter pilot. On Lenton Boulevard the vacant land on the west side was used for the handsome offices of the Raleigh Cycle Company, Lenton and Radford branch library, St Paul's Roman Catholic church and All Souls parish hall. On the opposite side, near Derby Road, the modern Cottesmore school was erected.

The City Council erected a new housing estate, Lenton Abbey, in the late 1920s at the western

Another building adjoining the University Park which has been demolished is the open-air swimming pool. New buildings erected on the site include a music school, art gallery, bookshop and restaurant.

boundary. In fact part of the estate was in the area of Beeston UDC until the council was able to adjust the boundary in 1932. Another small council estate was at Abbey Bridge, where a bridge over the railway improved communication with the city. The 1930s saw the construction of two important examples of modern architecture, for two of Nottingham's employers. John Player Limited, whose main factories were in Radford, built the tall bonded warehouses on Ilkeston Road, while Boots started to move some of its manufacturing premises to a site which straddled the border with Beeston near the Beeston Canal.

After World War Two, an early start was made on clearance of some of Lenton's unfit houses, with small schemes at Spring Close and around the Priory Street area. A much larger scheme followed which involved most of the original New Lenton area centred on Willoughby Street. This area was redeveloped with five multi-storey blocks of flats.

The early post-war years saw a policy by the City Council of controlled tipping on land formerly used for agriculture and allotments. After the building of the Clifton estate and a new bridge over the River Trent, Clifton Boulevard was extended as far as the bridge and formed part of the A52 road, which was diverted from Gamston so that it by-passed the centre of the city. Both sides of the new Clifton Boulevard were developed with commercial industrial and other buildings. On the south-west side, Players moved from Radford to a new Horizon tobacco factory. Also on this side a multi-screen cinema and a bowling alley were built. On the north side Gregory Street was widened and extended as Lenton Lane to join the A52. A large building on this side is the Central TV studios, now Carlton TV, which has used the district for much outdoor location work. A new road, Thane Road from the A52, crossed the Beeston Canal and ended at the city portion of Boots' Beeston site. An interesting episode in Lenton's history in the 1960s was the building of a small landing strip near

Poplars Road. This was used for an experimental helicopter service to Leicester, but was not a success.

The granting of university status to the former college was followed by an expansion of the campus. The Portland Building was built for students' social functions and a new Hallward library was erected. Other education buildings have been built towards Clifton Boulevard, with a multi-storey block for science subjects. The former lido has disappeared and been replaced by arts centres. The pavilion at the end of the lake has also been demolished and a new award-winning building erected, which incorporates a restaurant, theatre, and exhibition rooms.

A major extension of the university's status was the building of a teaching hospital, which incorporated some of the city's older hospitals and is known as the Queen's Medical Centre. Finally, a new part of the university has been built adjoining the Lenton part of the Wollaton Park estate and the Jubilee Campus celebrates the Queen's Jubilee. The southeastern side of University Boulevard has been developed with a science park and a tennis centre of national standard.

In 1884, J.T. Godfrey published his *History of*

The multi-storey flats at Willoughby Street, built in the 1960s, can be seen from the new bridge over the Nottingham Canal.

the Parish and Priory of Lenton in 499 pages. As will be seen in the bibliography referred to in the introduction the subsequent history has been supplemented, there being 32 references to Lenton. A number of these refer to Lenton Local History Society, which has produced a magazine since 1979. A Lenton trail dealing with the present day Old Lenton and its buildings has been produced by City Planning and Development. A recent publication by F.A. Barnes slightly exceeds Godfrey's number of pages. Entitled *Priory Demesne to University Campus* it gives a great deal of Lenton's history. It is listed under University of Nottingham in the bibliography.

MAPPERLEY

In mediaeval times, many surnames were the names of places, presumably where the holder came from, and were often preceded by 'de', meaning 'of'. One such man, Thomas de Mapperley, is mentioned in a legal dispute in Nottingham in 1483. However, it is considered that he had come from a place called Mapperley in Derbyshire and the district of Nottinghamshire was so called because he owned land there, probably in Basford parish, and his name was given to it, rather than the other way about.

Dr Thoroton in 1676 refers to the land being called Mapperley Closes and states that there was a cottage house or two and some odd barns erected 'it goes for a small hamlet called Mapperley'. The district's name only really becomes of significance with the Basford Enclosure Act of 1792. The closes were in Basford parish, adjoining the borough of Nottingham near the point where Arnold, Basford, Gedling and Nottingham meet. This northeastern part of the borough, known as Mapperley Hills from its elevation, remained entirely undeveloped

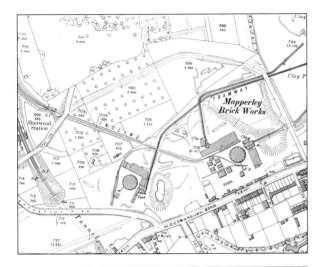

The tram terminus on Woodborough Road marked the city boundary. The building on the left is the Methodist church opened in 1903. The chimney beyond is at the brick works.

whole of the area covered about 500 acres, the south half having only one building on it, Mapperley House (later Hall), built for the Wright family in around 1792. On the borough side of Woodborough Road there was only a narrow strip no more than 100 yards wide reaching about three quarters of a mile to the boundary. On Jackson's map, based on surveys between 1851 and 1861, the only buildings shown are a small group of houses described as Mapperley Park. It was later renamed Alexandra Park and was a small private estate started in 1854 with large detached houses, there being no through road, mainly because the land to the east fell away sharply while to the south were the Hungerhill Gardens.

Blyth Street runs parallel to Woodborough Road from Ransom Road. The detached houses on the west side were erected in around 1910.

until the mid-19th century. On Sanderson's map of 1835 a number of brick-kilns are shown on the Basford side of the road to Woodborough with just one on the Nottingham side. The hills were the scene in 1842 of a large assembly of rioters, known as Chartists, who were seeking a charter to give the working classes greater rights.

Sanderson's map also shows the beginnings of the Sherwood district following the enclosure award. On the east side of the Mansfield Road, the northern boundary of Basford was Swinehouse Lane, now Woodthorpe Drive, and the southern boundary with the borough was known as Red Lane, later to be dignified as Redcliffe Road. Both the two boundary roads sloped upwards towards the borough boundary, Woodborough Road. The

Development along Woodborough Road started a few years later, on the east side, and by 1881 there were about 40 buildings beyond Alexandra Park stretching as far as the borough boundary, in small groups with gaps between. There were also two public houses, the Duke of Cambridge and the Belle Vue. They are still there but are modern rebuildings. There were also two new streets, Quernaby Road and Blyth Street, and a post office. The next 20 years saw the completion of building along the east side as far as Porchester Road, with other new streets with mainly working class houses. After 1877 the distinction between Mapperley and Sherwood became less relevant as both were then in

On the east side of Blyth Street is a large house of about the same period with a tower that commands wide views.

the Borough. Development on the east side was sporadic, as the land fell away and because of the continued use of the brickworks. These had been taken over by Edward Gripper as the Nottingham Brick Company. He was a man who devoted much of his life to public affairs, becoming an alderman of the borough council and mayor for one year. The great expansion of Nottingham led to most of the bricks used coming from these brickworks, leading to the saying 'Nottingham was built on Mapperley Hills'. In 1887 the vast Mapperley Mental Hospital was built near the junction of Woodborough Road and Porchester Road.

A more modest group of small houses is Agnes Villas, between Querneby Road and Woodborough Road. It is not open to traffic.

The 20th century saw electric trams running along Woodborough Road as far as the city boundary despite the steep gradients. These were later to be much more of a problem when buses and

cars used to come to a halt in severe winters. The Majestic Cinema on Woodborough Road, like most suburban cinemas, did not survive the television era but the building remains for commercial use. The brickworks too disappeared, although as late as the 1960s a chain-hauled light railway used to bring clay under Woodthorpe Drive from Arnold.

So near to busy roads, this peaceful scene is one of the approaches to Elliot Durham School.

Mapperley today is a mainly Victorian and Edwardian residential area. Most of Mapperley Hospital has been demolished and the sites and former grounds used for modern housing. Behind the buildings on Woodborough Road lies an almost rural scene down as far as St Ann's, with two modern schools with playing fields.

Alexandra Park off Woodborough Road has a number of large Victorian houses including this one, Springfield.

Perhaps inspired by the Nottingham Park and Alexandra Park developments the west side from Sherwood southwards has become Mapperley Park.

Malvern House on Mapperley Road has some decorative features including the gate pillars. From the rear it looks down on Mapperley Park.

This development was to extend over a period of 70 years, the initial stages being dependent upon what happened to Mapperley Hall. Ichabod Wright, who had the Hall built, lived to the age of 96, dying in 1862. Ichabod Charles, his eldest son, lived at the

Another distinctive house at the corner of Magdala Road and Mansfield Road is now a hotel.

Hall after his father died, but only until 1869. He leased the Hall and its grounds to Edward Manlove, lace manufacturer, for a short time, then leased to William Lambert, another manufacturer, who was an alderman and mayor of Nottingham in 1874. He stayed there for 10 years until 1888. In the meantime Colonel Charles Ichabod Wright, whose father Ichabod Charles had died in 1871, had started as early as 1873 to release lands not part of the Hall grounds, an advertisement referring to Magdala Road and Lucknow Drive.

Some of the smaller houses in Mapperley Park, such as this one on Alvestone Road, reflect the more restrained later houses.

However, the first houses do not appear to have been built until 1881, by which time Mapperley Park was in the borough. After Lambert left the Hall, Colonel Wright and his son Charles Bingham Wright lived in Mapperley Hall, although Colonel Wright had another house in Torquay. In the 20 years up to 1900, 95 detached houses, all designed by well-known architects, had been built in the southern part of the estate, mainly on Magdala, Redcliffe and Zulla Roads. The houses had to comply with restrictions imposed by a sale of the land agreement, which included that they must be of a value of at least £800. There was an open space off Mansfield Road, which had been acquired by the Nottingham Boys' High School for a cricket ground. In 1877 a new church building was started in the north-east corner of the estate, although it was not completed until 1929.

A significant change took place in 1903 when the Wright family sold the Hall and extensive grounds by auction, a total of 129 acres, for £74,000. It was purchased by a syndicate of businessmen; J.B. Derbyshire, S.P. Derbyshire and John Ashworth. An architect, William Beedham Starr, later joined the syndicate and designed many of the subsequent houses.

In 1904 a development plan for the new part of the estate was approved, involving nine new streets, one of which was Mapperley Hall Drive. From then onwards many applications for new houses were approved, reaching a total of 484 by 1912. Not all these were built, including the largest number submitted as one scheme, 56. This was perhaps no great loss as the scheme has been described as 'terrible' for its layout and quality of the houses.

By 1910 the total number occupied was 410, the number of applications for approval being much smaller in the years up to the outbreak of the war, by which time there were 500 houses altogether. It was thus a mainly Edwardian suburb and many of the houses showed the influence of contemporary architects such as Charles Voysey and others, creating the so-called 'Queen Anne' style. Mapperley Hall itself was bought by Nottingham City Council as a hostel for students at the nearby University College.

No new houses were built during the 1914–18

Seen from Tavistock Drive is the sports ground, first owned by Nottingham Girls' High School, which later became the police training ground, with houses in the background on Esher Grove.

period, but there was still much available land and in the period 1919–39 a further 200 were built, mainly single houses by a large number of different architects. A block of four flats was built in this period as well as the first division of one house into two flats.

During World War Two Mapperley Hall was used as the headquarters of the North Midland Region for Civil Defence. After the war it was used as the headquarters offices for the electricity and water authorities. More recently it has been converted into flats with other dwelling accommodation in the adjoining grounds. Mapperley Park is one of the city's conservation areas and it has an active residents association.

NEW BASFORD

As mentioned in the chapter on Basford parish, the increasing population in the early 19th century was due largely to the development of the local trade, in Nottingham and the adjacent villages. This started as a result of technical changes based on the stocking frame. The main change was introduced by John Heathcote, who perfected a machine that made true lace, which could not be made on stocking frames. What became known as 'bobbin

net' or 'twist net' fever saw a rapid increase in the number of the new machines. The four former villages, which adjoined the borough, took advantage of this to create new settlements as near to the borough as possible.

In Basford's case this was a new village, separated by about a mile from the old one. The name New Basford first appears in the baptismal registers of the parish church of St Leodegarius in

From near the junction with Duke Street, Mount Street slopes downwards. In 1962 clearance of some of the first houses built in the 1820s began.

The Baptist chapel on Palm Street was erected in 1852 but was demolished in order to permit redevelopment of the area.

This block on Duke Street had the classical pediment with its date stone of 1853.

Radford Road and Gawthorne Street and extended northwards as far as North Gate. *White's Directory* of 1832 describes New Basford as 'a large village, which has been raised in the last 10 years and consists of several good streets which cross each other at right angles and are occupied principally by bobbin net makers'. The directory lists 140 bobbin net makers' names in the whole parish of Basford, of whom 48 were in New Basford. The 1841 census revealed that there were 441 houses with a population of 1,218. The next 10 years saw almost a doubling of the number of people to 2,343 souls. The names of the streets included George Street, King Street, Pepper Street and Chapel Street, which were changed after 1877 when Basford became part of the borough. This was because the names duplicated ones in Nottingham. The street pattern still remains the same today, apart from a few changes. *White's Directory* of 1853 gives a picture of the changes, which had taken place in the previous years. 'Here is a room fitted up for divine service belonging to the Church of England. A district church will be erected as soon as sufficient funds can be raised. The Baptists, General Baptists, Wesleyan, Wesleyan Association and Primitive Methodists have each a chapel here. Here is a reading room and library, established 3rd November 1848 and contains 260 volumes'. The same directory gives a separate list of the principal inhabitants and tradesmen. There were 40 in the

1813 when the addresses of 19 of the parents were given as New Basford but without a street name. The first houses and streets were on 30 acres of land which were sold by Abigail Gawthorne in 1814. This was in the south of the parish up to the borough boundary. It lay between what is today

The clearance of the houses opened up extensive views northwards. This one shows North Gate in the right-hand corner and the gas works to the left, most of which has been demolished.

first category, including two farmers, an accountant, two bookkeepers, a solicitor's clerk and a collector of highway rates.

New Basford had been made a new benefice on 4 October 1848 and the Revd Thomas Ambler Bolton became the first incumbent. The room referred to in the 1853 directory was in Olive Square and was rented at 1s 6d a week. Fifteen years later a new church dedicated to St Augustine was built on the street, which was later renamed High Church Street.

The suburb continued to grow, the population in 1901 being 8,061. To house the increased numbers, the district had expanded eastwards as far as Nottingham Road and north of North Gate as far as Fairfax Street. Two new streets were given names derived from the wars in South Africa – Zulu Road and Isandula Road. The south-east corner of the suburb extending as far as Nottingham Road became mainly residential, and still exists much the same as when it was first built. Adjoining it was a large lace factory for Thomas Adams Limited, whose warehouse had been built in Nottingham's Lace Market. This building later became part of John Player and Sons tobacco business until it was demolished and a new Djanogly Technology College built on the site.

The extent to which New Basford had become industrialised by 1892 is illustrated by a map drawn up then. This was a section of Goad's insurance map, which was produced to help insurance companies evaluate the properties for which they were asked to issue policies. The large scale, 40ft to one inch, gives the location of every property in the area surveyed, with different colours for various classes of properties. Houses are marked D, while factories with roof lights have them marked blue. The names of the occupiers of industrial premises are given and the number of storeys each had.

An interesting caption is appended to a vacant site at the corner of North Gate and Rawson Street, which it describes as Ward and Cope's fire brigade.

It consisted of 13 men, drilled and equipped with hydrants and hose distributors.

The importance of the lace industry to New Basford can be seen in the list of the firms at the end of the 19th century in a directory for 1902. This gave the names of lace manufacturers amounting to 270 in Nottingham and its suburbs. Of these six were in New Basford, of which four were limited companies. Manufacturers were those who not only had factories making lace but who also carried out the commercial side involving finishing processes and selling and distribution. Another list of 200 names were described as lace makers (machine holders). These were smaller concerns who rented space in 20 tenement factories. There were five of these in New Basford, three of them on High Church Street, one of them, Simpson's, having 10 tenants.

The southern edge of New Basford was developed later in the 19th century with some well-built houses such as these on Alma Street.

Other industries in the area included five hosiery factories and John Jardine's bobbin, carriage and cycle maker, jacquard and lace machine builder. James Shipstone and Sons Limited, brewery, occupied a large area on Radford Road extending back to Rawson Street, including houses for employees. One street and terrace were named Shipstone.

The growth of the district had seen the rise to local fame of a number of men, who at first lived in the area close to their work places. Foremost among these was Richard Birkin. He came from Belper in Derbyshire as one of the earliest lace manufacturers in the 1820s, when he was 20 years old, and prospered so well that he was able in 1853 to move to the Lace Market in Nottingham, where he built a large new warehouse involving creating a new street called Broadway. The buildings were designed by the Nottingham architect T.C. Hine and are still there as one of the Lace Market's listed buildings.

This small industrial building on Radford Road was built in 1904 for a gas meter manufacturer.

At first he lived in Mount Street, but by 1850 he was sufficiently wealthy to buy a country residence, Aspley Hall, on the outskirts of Nottingham. He was an alderman of the Borough Council. He was also the leader of the dominant Liberal Party on the council and a Conservative member of the council who kept a diary once went to see him. In his diary he recounts that the main reason for the visit was to discuss how the two parties could prevent a certain Liberal councillor from being elected as mayor on the grounds that his habit of frequenting ale houses was not in keeping with the dignity of the office. William Parsons, the diarist, also used the opportunity to buy some pigs from Richard Birkin. The latter was himself appointed mayor on four occasions, while Parsons became the first Conservative to hold that office.

Richard Birkin also became a director of the

Midland Railway and when he died in 1870 he left what was then a sizeable fortune of £35,000. He married twice and his second wife died two days after him. One of his sons, Thomas Isaac, was born at New Basford in 1832 and carried on the lace business his father had started. He continued to live on Pepper Street (the name was later changed to Palm Street). The business continued to expand and when he was created a baronet he, like his father, moved to a country house, Ruddington Grange. He had several children and the baronetcy passed on through one of his sons and is still in existence. Subsequent generations included a number of men who became well known in Nottinghamshire, including a racing car driver who died in the 1930s. Others have had distinguished military careers while a female descendant, Jane, became a noted actress and singer. The family name survives in Nottingham through Birkin Avenue.

Another New Basford man who created one of Nottingham's most famous breweries was James Shipstone. He died in 1898 and also left a considerable fortune of £47,000. He had a large family and his sons carried on the business, including Thomas, who was subsequently given a knighthood. One of his daughters became Mrs V. Snell, who wrote a book of reminiscences in which she recounted Sir Thomas's sense of humour. On one occasion she and her sisters had been to a social occasion and were to be collected by the family's coachman driving the carriage. Sir Thomas himself disguised himself as the coachman and created no little alarm when he drove the carriage in the opposite way to home.

Wallis Binch, a lace manufacturer who lived in Beech Avenue near to his factory for a time, became Lord Mayor of Nottingham in 1939.

New Basford was connected with Nottingham Corporation in the 19th and early 20th centuries. In 1854 Nottingham Gas Light and Coke Company constructed a gas works between Basford Road and the railway. The company was taken over by the

Corporation in 1874 and the works became a major employer in the area as the Gas Department supplied a large area outside the city as well as the city itself.

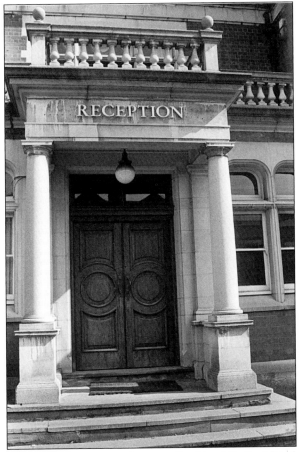

Shipstone's brewery on the opposite side of Radford Road was built up from small beginnings and had a handsome reception office which is still in use for its new owners.

The Corporation Water Department also had an interest for a time at New Basford. Like gas, water supply had been undertaken by a private company, which erected a works at Scotholme Meadow to supply water from the River Leen. The company was also taken over in 1880 and on the advice of the Medical Officer of Health, who had found the supply polluted, Scotholme was closed.

The Corporation started its tram system in 1901 and a line was established through New Basford. In the early days the generation of electricity for this purpose was first of all used to recharge large batteries, as this could take place at night when the trams were not running. In 1911 an electric battery power sub-station was built on Isandula Road. When the trams finished in 1936 the building continued to be used as an electricity sub-station.

The first half of the 20th century saw little change in the area. A small scheme of council houses was built in Liddington Street and a swimming pool and wash house was erected on the edge of the district on Noel Street. The lace industry was declining and by 1941 one of the tenement factories had as tenants a leather bag manufacturer, a lithographic printer, a fancy goods manufacturer and a manufacturing chemists. There were still four lace manufacturers as tenants.

New Basford clearance area has been redeveloped for industry, with modern workshops and warehouses such as these at the bottom of Palm Street.

A major change in New Basford affecting most of the original settlement was inaugurated in 1960 when the City Council made a compulsory purchase order. This was primarily to deal with the houses between John Street and Gawthorne Street. Some of these were 130 years old and of a standard which precluded any form of improvement. Other houses and properties, although not unfit, were included where necessary to form a site suitable for development. Most of the existing industrial buildings were not included in the order. A redevelopment plan accompanied the order, which indicated that new houses were not to be built, as had been the case in other clearance areas. Instead, the area was to become mainly industrial. Some streets were to be partially closed off. The redevelopment took place gradually with mainly modern-style units, which could be adapted for different uses as required.

Today the appearance of the area presents a different picture than it did, with trees, open spaces, and a new school with adjoining playing field. The brewery complex was not affected by the clearance scheme but has undergone a radical change. The brewery has gone and has been replaced in part by a firm of auctioneers. Other parts have been demolished and new dwellings erected on the site. The large tower, a prominent landmark, has been retained.

The remainder of New Basford from North Gate to Fairfax Street has remained largely unchanged, apart from some streets being closed to vehicles. On the west side of Radford Road, the coming of North Sea Gas has resulted in the demolition of the former gas works. The site is now awaiting proposals for new development. The new rapid transport tram system will only directly affect New Basford where it runs parallel to the railway, but it will be on the perimeter along Radford Road.

THE PARK

Nottingham has three residential suburbs defined as 'parks', all created as such in the 19th century. While two are known as Alexandra Park and Mapperley Park, the third is more usually known as The Park, although for official or legal purposes it is either Nottingham Park, or the Park Estate, Nottingham. It does have some justification for the seemingly exclusive appellation since it has been a park since early mediaeval times. The term 'park' has been in more general use since the 19th century as a description of often municipal recreation grounds. Its earlier meaning referred to the setting aside of part of a land-holding, often attached to an aristocrat's house, and implied the enclosing or keeping private of the part. In mediaeval times the Crown looked with disfavour on any member of the nobility seeming to rival the monarch, who in legal terms owned the whole of the country, and permission was required to 'empark'.

In Nottingham such permission was not required as the land now known as The Park had been royal property since Norman times. After the Norman William became King of England, his followers were rewarded with grants of land throughout the kingdom, one object of which was to enable them to control or suppress the Anglo-Saxon inhabitants. In Nottingham William Peverel, the King's natural son, erected a motte and bailey castle on the easily defendable 130ft high rock. This copied the similar foundation across the valley at the Anglo-Saxon burh (borough). The motte and bailey was later replaced by a permanent castle, which became a royal palace for some 500 years. The two boroughs, the English and the French, the latter extending eastwards, eventually became a united borough.

Some of the earliest houses in the Park are the semi-detached villas on Park Terrace.

Stucco was used to a great extent in the early stages, as on these elegant houses on Park Valley.

To the west of the castle the open country was 'emparked' to become a royal enclosure used for the sport of the King and his retinues, who were to use the castle on occasions during the succeeding centuries. It was part of the royal Sherwood Forest, which had a similar function and the deer and other game would occupy the whole.

Brick, with polychromatic courses and features such as finials, was favoured in later years by Watson Fothergill on this house on Newcastle Drive.

By the beginning of the 17th century the castle and its park were no longer needed by the Crown and were sold to the Earl of Rutland. The castle was not in a good state of repair but it served as a stronghold for the Parliamentary forces in the civil wars. The governor, Colonel Hutchinson, eventually ordered its demolition and after the restoration of the monarch, Charles II, the site was purchased by William Cavendish, Earl of

Newcastle, who for his adherence to the Royalist cause was made the 1st Duke of Newcastle. In 1674 he started to build his new mansion, which he insisted on calling Nottingham Castle. This has led to disgruntled visitors to Nottingham complaining to this day that it has no battlements or towers and is not what they expect a castle to look like.

The land to the west was re-enclosed and restocked with deer as the private garden of the new mansion. The first Duke died in 1679 and as he had no male heir the estate went to his nephew Thomas Pelham Holles. Following further failure of the male line the estate passed to another nephew Henry Pelham Clinton. These surnames, together with others from other families that subsequent dukes married into, are perpetuated in the road names of The Park.

Houses with half timbering on Tattershall Drive are much lower than the houses in the background.

In the late 18th century, the castle ceased to be a residence of the ducal owners and was let as apartments. The adjoining park came to be regarded as a place for the town's inhabitants to visit for fresh air and a rural scene, especially as Nottingham was becoming more and more overcrowded. This was to be a bone of contention in the future, as various plans were drawn up to develop The Park. The 3rd Duke of Newcastle, the title having been recreated for his grandfather, started the disposal of part of the estate by giving one acre of the land for the erection of Nottingham General Hospital, which was built in 1780 on land just outside the borough boundary. In 1792 a barracks was erected on part of The Park, on its western edge adjoining what is now Barrack Lane, leading off Derby Road. A former fishpond at the southern end was filled in and let as gardens. Inhabitants of the town were allowed to graze animals on payment of a fee.

The former mews, backing onto the castle rock, have been converted to living accommodation.

The Park, which measured about half a mile west of the castle, was bounded by Derby Road on the north and the borough boundary on the east. The land sloped steeply southwards and westwards from the two boundaries and also from the barracks, down to the foot road to Lenton and the River Leen. The Normans had diverted the Leen to the foot of the castle, until it was incorporated into the Nottingham Canal. It therefore formed a bowl. The castle and its environs, including The Park and land to the north of the castle as far as Derby Road were, as a royal domain, not attached to a parish and were known as extra-parochial with freedom from parochial rates. It was described as the 'Castle and Liberties'.

When the 3rd Duke died in 1785, his son the 4th Duke was only 10 years old, so the estate was managed for his mother the dowager Duchess by trustees. In any case, the Duke was foolish enough to visit France in 1803, regardless of the fact that England was at war with the French. He was interned there and apparently grew to hate the

egalitarian ideas of the French after the revolution. This, and his natural arrogance, led to him become, like many of his aristocratic and land-owning compatriots, a reactionary die-hard opponent of reform. He opposed the Reform Bill in 1832, which sought to modernise the electoral system. This in turn was responsible for a mob in Nottingham burning down his castle, which was to remain a roofless ruin until 1875.

The horse can no longer enjoy grazing on Lincoln Circus as it has been converted into a rest garden.

After the Duke had returned to England in 1807 about two acres of land on Standard Hill, part of the Liberties, was sold for a superior development of houses and for a new church, St James's. In the 1830s the first houses in what can be regarded as The Park proper were erected on Derby Road at Western Terrace and in the lower part at Park Valley.

Various plans had been drawn up from time to time, which did not come to fruition until after the 4th Duke died and was succeeded by his son, Pelham Fiennes Clinton. One of the earlier plans had shown a rectangular grid pattern and another showed a proposed church which never materialised. In 1854 a revised plan was adopted, and the layout remains largely unaltered. A local architect, Thomas Chambers Hine, was appointed surveyor to the estate. He designed many of the houses in The Park and was later responsible for renovating the castle for Nottingham Corporation as an art gallery and museum.

The final plan, no doubt influenced by some of those cities in the south such as Bath, Cheltenham and London, included two circular open spaces connected by a walk, called Newcastle and Lincoln Circuses. Surrounding them were oval shaped crescents. One main entrance was just outside the castle entrance and along Lenton Road, a straight thoroughfare across the south part of The Park. It had been made at a less steep gradient by removing tons of rock. Another entrance led on to Derby Road at the north-west corner.

The tennis courts were used for some years for a pre-Wimbledon tournament.

A feature that had been planned for years was finally completed in 1855, a tunnel on a low level on the east side to Derby Road. This was intended so that horse-drawn carriages could avoid steeper gradients to Derby Road. Unfortunately, it was found that the exit to Derby Road was itself too steep for the horses and so it remained a pedestrian exit. The labour of constructing the tunnel so impressed the Duke that he gave a dinner to the workmen, costing £5.

The houses to be built had to be of a minimum size and value, with strict covenants to ensure that The Park remained an exclusive area for the wealthier classes. Many had large gardens and were of a size that could accommodate large Victorian families and servants. As well as Hine, other outstanding Nottingham architects such as Watson Fothergill and Arthur Marshall designed houses.

Tree planting was a feature of the layout and street lighting was by gas, as it still is. Building continued spasmodically until the early years of the 20th century.

W.E. Gladstone, the Victorian Prime Minister, indulged in one of his hobbies, felling trees, on a visit to the Park, a cross-section being incorporated into the structure on Tunnel Road.

Although extra-parochial parishes were abolished by an Act of Parliament in 1868, the Castle and Liberties, including The Park, remained outside the jurisdiction of the borough until 1877. The borough then introduced its extension bill, which sought to include The Park as well as the other adjoining parishes. The wealthy inhabitants could afford proper legal advice and were able to secure advantages, including the right to maintain the private nature of the estate by continuing to be responsible for their own roads, lighting and sewers. In return they were given a discount from the borough rates, as the borough was saved expenses. They were also able to insist that the estate continued to approve all plans instead of submitting them to the Corporation.

When the 5th Duke died his heir was a minor and trustees were appointed to oversee the management of the estate. One of these was William Ewart Gladstone, several times Prime Minister. On one of his visits to The Park, he indulged in one of his favourite pastimes, felling trees. A cross section of a trunk of one he felled was incorporated in an iron plaque with appropriate wording. One house was named Gladstone.

Tunnel Road led to the exit from the Park to Derby Road.

By the first decade of the 20th century some of The Park's attractions for the wealthy were being eroded. Other similar estates had been established in the city (as the borough became in 1897) and the increasing use of motor cars enabled some to seek

Another steep exit is the flight of steps from Park Valley to Park Row.

houses in the country around the city, such as Plumtree Park and Manor Park at Ruddington. After World War One economic and social conditions had their effect on The Park. The decline of the textile industries, especially lace, and the growing trend for smaller families resulted in the large Park houses becoming less desirable. Another factor was that the houses had been built on 99-year leases and some were already 70 years old in the 1930s. Houses in The Park could be bought relatively cheaply, and some were converted into flats. Coach houses could be converted to garages or even into living accommodation.

World War Two and its aftermath did not help matters. Shortage of materials and the increasing age of the houses made it difficult to keep the houses in good repair. Some sold off parts of their large gardens for the erection of new dwellings or were converted into unsatisfactory flats. Cars became an increasing problem, both because of the number of them using The Park as a through route and because of residents' parking. Some economic relief for residents came in 1952, when the Oxford University Chest, which had purchased the estate, allowed them to convert the 99-year leases to freehold.

Another important change came in 1968 when a Civic Amenities Act was passed. This enabled local authorities to set up conservation areas. These enabled planning authorities to insist on any future development in them being of a form which enhanced the status of the buildings and their environment. The City Council made The Park a conservation area and the Department of the Environment pronounced it an area of outstanding importance in the national context. By 1980, 29 of the buildings in The Park were listed as having architectural or historic merit. A review of the city's list of such buildings in 1998 added a further 36 to the list.

A Park Residents' Association has been formed to safeguard the area's uniqueness and the city's Planning and Development Department has issued guidance on how its status can be retained. Today, parking restrictions have been imposed and barriers at entrances help to control vehicle traffic. It is a pity that visitors who are disappointed with the castle do not take the trouble to visit this unique feature of Nottingham's history.

RADFORD

Like its neighbours Basford and Lenton, Radford was an Anglo-Saxon settlement on the River Leen. In the Domesday Book, spelled Redeforde in Latin, it had land for nine ploughs with 15 families, with four mills and half a fishery showing how it made use of its position on the River Leen. It seems to

The former workhouse on St Peter's Street survived as houses until the 1960s.

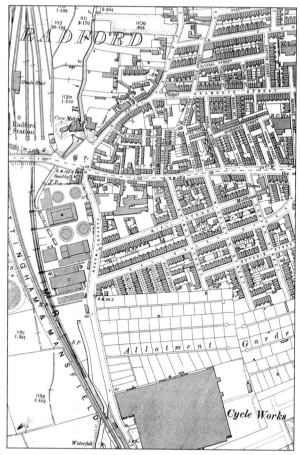

while 613 to 636 are named as 'in or near Lenton cum Radford'. The map shows buildings, in a line parallel to the River Leen, on a street stretching about 170 yards. It shows Mr Collinson's mill and, about half a mile north of the main part of the town, Bavers Mill, with a drawing of a bridge over the river. This is no doubt Bobbers Mill, first recorded in 1335 as Boberismilne.

The early 19th-century house on Alfreton Road still has the original top storey long window for the stocking frame knitters.

have been slightly larger than its neighbour Lenton, but Dr Thoroton in his book of 1676 tells us that William Peverel, who owned Radford as well as many other places, 'gave this Town to the Monastery he founded at Lenton with which it was ever mixed and so continues.' The monastery was a priory of the Cluniac order founded in 1102–8. It was dissolved in the 16th century and so for over 400 years Radford was really very much a part of Lenton.

After the priory was dissolved, Radford would have become a more independent parish with its church, dedicated to St Peter, having been rebuilt in 1812. In 1609 a survey of the lands of Sherwood Forest was carried out, detailing each separate parcel of land with descriptions of homes of freeholders and tenants. A map was drawn up covering both Lenton and Radford. Each parcel of land is numbered, 599 to 612 being wholly Lenton

The Protestation Return of 1641 lists 77 adult men with 58 names. Surnames Matthews, Crampton, and Ward also appear in the names in the 1609 survey. Robert Malam was named in the return but he was absent, although he subsequently attested along with the officials of Rushcliffe Hundreds. Francis Beard of Esple, being a recusant (Catholic) 'hath not taken this protestation'. He and his wife had both been presented, that is, summoned before the consistory Court as not

Radford Folly was an 18th-century refinement, a provincial attempt to copy the London attractions of places like the Vauxhall Gardens. The industrialisation of Radford, including the sinking of a colliery, meant that it had a sad end as a coal wharf. (LSL)

having attended church. Aspley Hall, as his residence Esple was otherwise known, was on the edge of the parish, although not shown on the 1609 map. Aspley is dealt with in a separate chapter.

Other documents which give names of persons in 1664 and 1674 are the Hearth Tax Returns for those years. Unfortunately the list for 1664 is incomplete and although Radford is included in the index, this refers to a place in Bassetlaw Hundred which was part of Worksop. The return for 1674 is more complete and includes several places in Broxtowe Hundred which are not in the 1664 return including Radford, Lenton and Wollaton. It is not possible therefore to compare Radford's 1674 return with that of 1664. It lists 38 names with 78 hearths. This shows Mr Bearde with 8 hearths, Mr Ripley with seven, Mr Mash six, Mr William Alvey five and three others with four, including Mr Parker, rector. The rest had mostly one hearth. Most of the names given do not appear in the Protestation return of 1641, 33 years earlier. This indicates that there was a considerable turnover of people. It is likely that there were more than 38 hearths in Radford in 1674, as the return does not list those

who were not liable for the Hearth Tax on account of poverty.

In 1793, when John Throsby issued a new edition of *Dr Thoroton's Antiquities*, he added a note of his own. He wrote 'The village is a little paradise; or rather, a portion of it in the possession of Mr Elliott of Nottingham'. This was Radford Folly, which Throsby describes as showing 'the conception of a large and chaste mind, so far as relates to embellishment and landscape'. The extensive pleasure grounds, he said, had 'water and various foliage happily blended in groups and temple forms'. In 1832 *White's Directory* refers to it as Radford Grove, 'a delightful place of public resort, planned and laid out at great expense in 1780, by the late William Elliott Esq.' The mansion was described as a commodious inn.

The directory goes on to describe Radford as 'having drank so deeply of the manufacturing spirit of Nottingham town that it now ranks as the second most populous parish in the county' that is, a larger population than Mansfield or Newark. The population had risen to 2,269 in 1801, more than doubled by 1821 and more than doubled again 10

The community spirit of Radford in the early 20th century is shown by this war memorial, paid for and erected by the inhabitants.

directory also listed the industrial concerns – 'three bleach works, two corn mills, an extensive cotton and worsted mill, two immense bobbin net manufactories, in one of which, the machines are worked by steam'.

The directory also listed the separate villages which had grown up in the last 20 or 30 years. These were New Radford, Hyson Green, Aspley, Bloomsgrove, Bobbers Mill, Kensington, Lovett Mills and Sherwood Hill. Hyson Green, mainly because of its size and subsequent growth, is dealt with in a separate chapter. Aspley at this time was described as a small hamlet, part of Lord Middleton's estate and consisted mainly of Aspley Hall. It remained more or less in this situation for a hundred years and has been mentioned in earlier chapters setting out the history of the group of villages which from the 1920s onward combined to form a major part of Nottingham's council housing estates.

years later. *White's Directory* quoted the number of houses in 1821 as 973, compared with 2,073 10 years later. The houses built in the 10 years from 1821 to 1831 'form several handsome villages, occupied mainly by bobbin net makers, the houses built with bricks and roofed with blue slates'. The

One of the large factories built when the home-based industries could no longer survive.

The increasing urbanisation of Radford, as elsewhere, led to problems of sanitation and hygiene. One reason was the lack of any proper control over standards of building, while enforcement of proper sanitary measures was minimal. The Government had passed an Act in 1848 to allow towns to form Local Boards of Health but Radford was slow to take such a step.

Radford Woodhouse was a small separate part of the district near the Nottingham Canal.

In 1871 the Medical Department of the Privy Council ordered an enquiry to be made into the prevalence of typhoid fever at Radford. A report was submitted by Dr Thorne, who carried out the enquiry, in which he said that there had been an epidemic of typhoid fever of unusual magnitude in the previous year with 300 cases and 26 deaths. Diarrhoea had also been prevalent, resulting in another 21 deaths. The main cause of disease was polluted water supplies from wells, due to inadequate sewage disposal.

Dr Thorne's report gives some horrifying details of living conditions in Radford at this time. 'In laying out the streets and yards the main object seems to have been to build the largest possible number of houses in the smallest possible space.' Houses were built back to back with no through ventilation. The worst feature was the privy midden system. There was no proper provision for the removal of their contents and for enforcing cleanliness, and they were sources of intolerable

nuisance and of great danger to public health. He concluded his report by saying that no locality of Radford's population should be without a Medical Officer of Health.

The following year he submitted a second report in which he was able to mention some improvement in measures to prevent further outbreaks of disease. He again criticised the parish for not having set up a Local Board of Health or appointed a Medical Officer of Health. He also accused the Board of Guardians of not carrying out its duty to ensure vaccination of infants. Another cause for complaint

Another small hamlet, Bobbers Mill, still has these 18th-century houses on Cyril Avenue.

was the failure to provide hospital accommodation for those suffering from infectious diseases. To illustrate the need he recounts the result of a visit he made to a house. The house was in a narrow dirty yard, dilapidated and unfit for habitation. In one room he found that eight people had slept there, but two had died in the previous fortnight. The six still there all occupied the same bed. In the same room there was a dead body and another had been there the previous week. A Local Board of Health was appointed in 1874 but before it was able to do very much it was dissolved when Radford became annexed to the borough in 1877.

The reasons for the borough extension are set out in the chapter on Basford. All the parishes which were so transferred then became subject to the town's system of requiring all proposals for new

Stilton Terrace, Neston Street, was typical of the houses with common gardens and factories nearby.

Near the border with the borough is one of the first Board schools, which still stands largely unaltered externally.

buildings and alterations to existing ones to be submitted to the council for approval. This ensured that all houses in future were properly constructed.

One of the ways in which Radford benefited from incorporation into the borough was the construction of the boulevard system. This consisted of four sections, which today are an important part of the by-passing of central Nottingham. This was equally important when they were first laid out as they enabled horse-drawn traffic to avoid the steep inclines of Derby Road and Ilkeston Road. Radford Boulevard was opened by 1886 and Gregory Boulevard, which was partly in Radford and partly in the borough, had been in use since 1883. These boulevards also opened up building land for further development. The linking up of the separate roads from the town to Bulwell also benefited Radford in a similar way.

One of the very first new buildings in Radford when it became part of the borough was a public

Industry has been given a modern appearance too, on Alfreton Road.

baths on Boden Street. This soon became so popular that an extension was called for. The headmaster of a local private school complained that because the bath could be used for a very low charge, it did not afford a sufficient guarantee to bathers of the upper classes of cleanliness and freedom from infection.

By 1901, when the population had risen to 35,000, Radford's 600 acres were almost completely built up. There were several large factories that had been built since 1877. Players Castle Tobacco factory was one, which even gave its name to Player Street, while a large tenement factory, the Boulevard Works on Radford Boulevard, had separate tenancies for lace machine holders. William Hollins had the large Radford Mill on Garden Street for textile manufacturing.

Radford had no doubt benefited from incorporation in some ways, particularly from the stronger regulation powers of the town as regards general matters affecting public health. The annual report of the General Works and Highways Committee of the council for 1896 reported that the streets in the busy parts of the town and in some of the poorer districts were disinfected during the hot weather by adding to the water used for watering a strong but non-poisonous disinfectant. Radford would no doubt have qualified as one of the poorer districts. Watering in those days was a necessity because of horse-drawn traffic.

Little could be done by the beginning of the 20th century to improve the general standard of living accommodation for the older parts of the city, Nottingham having had this status conferred in 1897. There was certainly awareness of the wretched conditions in some parts, especially from members of the medical professions, the clergy and some of the socially conscious better-off classes. The connection between unhealthy houses and yards and sickness and high death rates was recognised. Attempts at improvement were limited by the lack of powers to enforce better conditions and by the financial considerations.

However, a new Act of Parliament affecting housing was passed and followed in Nottingham by the setting-up in 1909 for the first time of a Housing Committee of the City Council. Its powers were limited, compared with those granted later, but a start was made in ways that were permitted. Less than a month after the first meeting of the committee, members met at the junction of Forest Road West and Alfreton Road. From there it was only a short distance to Parker Street in Radford. As a result of the committee's visit the Medical Officer of Health was instructed to report on the properties on the south side of the street. He soon prepared his report and the committee had to decide what action to take against houses that were unfit. The owner could be ordered to demolish them, or to cease using them as houses, or could do such works as were possible to render them fit.

The committee was informed that an owner of property in Deakins Yard, Radford, had agreed to demolish some obstructive buildings and to build new water closets and wash houses at a cost of £470. The committee agreed to pay the owner a sum of £150 towards the work. The Housing Committee carried on this sort of action each year up to 1914.

Writing in 1914, Robert Mellors in his book *Radford and Hyson Green – Then and Now*, mentioned how the part of Radford around Parker

Street was not an inviting one, but praised the way it had been improved. Most important of all, he commented, was that 'the houses are let only to

This tranquil oasis on busy Ilkeston Road was formerly the site of Christ Church.

decent people and the ladies working with Miss H. Carey at the Social Guild exercise a benevolent oversight.' He later wrote 'there is district in Radford which has a knick-name which has been given, symbolical of sin, vice and crime.' He refrained from mentioning the name, Sodom and Gomorrah, but said the appellation was unjust as its inhabitants were not worse than other people. He did say that there were in various districts 'those who had neither the fear of God nor regard for man, an annoyance to their neighbours.'

From 1920 onwards the City Council was engaged in building a large number of council houses. Radford had two estates at the west end of Ilkeston Road, one at Kennington Road and the other on both sides of the southern end of the new ring road, Western Boulevard. The City Council also embarked on schemes of slum clearance, but these were mainly in the area of the old borough. After World War Two, priority was given to building council houses mainly on undeveloped land. It was not until 1955 that the Government allowed slum clearance to begin again.

In December of that year the City Council received a report from the Housing Committee seeking clearance and compulsory purchase orders

The Woodlands group of high-rise flats has been given a face-lift and is a landmark for miles around.

for the first large scheme. Entitled the Denman Street scheme, it involved a large area of Radford, starting at Canning Circus and triangular in shape extending northwards between Ilkeston Road and Alfreton Road as far as Independent Street. The scheme was to include the unfit houses, a limited number of properties adjoining them, and also a new category. This was under powers contained in the Housing Act 1949, which introduced grants to housing authorities and other owners to improve sound houses which had no modern amenities, such as bathrooms, indoor toilets and proper food stores. The scheme did not include acquisitions of factories, commercial buildings or most shops and public houses, mainly because of the cost. However, the proposals for the acquisition and improvement of houses were not approved by the government and a revised scheme was submitted.

Proposals were submitted for the building of dwellings on the cleared sites. Because of the costs and the need to maximise the number of dwellings on them, the City Council for the first time decided to build high-rise flats for most of the area. As at Old Basford and other areas, the high-rise flats were not popular at first. Other clearance areas in Radford were declared later until the re-development of most of the area extended to Hartley Road and Radford Boulevard. Unfortunately, one particular area, consisting of four blocks called Bampton, Bladon, Broadway and Buckland Courts, containing 375 flats, became the target of vandals, criminals and anti-social tenants. The flats became so notorious that the City Council spent £20 million on an estate action scheme, which refurbished the flats, introduced security controls and landscaped the surrounding area. The names of the blocks were changed to names of trees and are now occupied by satisfied tenants.

Radford has changed in recent years in other ways. The large tobacco factory on Radford Boulevard was demolished when Players moved to a new factory on Clifton Boulevard. Other old industrial buildings have been replaced by modern premises.

SHERWOOD

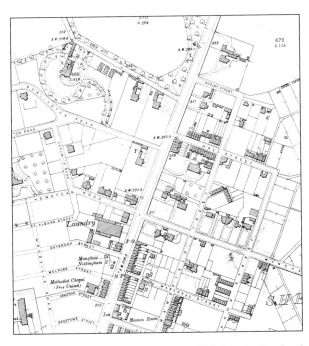

In 1832 *White's Directory* recorded that in Basford parish a number of new villages had been established in recent years, due to the increasing population of Nottingham and its surrounding districts. The increase in population was not just a natural increase in existing families but from families coming in from elsewhere attracted by work in the textile industries. This had a knock-on effect as houses had to be built to accommodate them and other occupations were needed to feed, clothe and supply other needs. In some cases accommodation for the population increase was met by merely expanding the boundaries of existing villages. This was not always possible, for various reasons such as the availability of suitable land and the price of it.

There were, however, other alternatives, especially in Basford's case, since it was a very large parish in acreage. Most of the land in the east of the parish was, as part of Sherwood Forest, undeveloped because of the poor quality of the land for arable agriculture. Moreover, a large part was

commonable, that is subject to ancient rights of inhabitants to graze cattle or cut turf for fuel or gather wild crops. This meant that the owners of the land could not use it to their best advantage.

As elsewhere in England in the 18th century, such rights of common were regarded as a hindrance to redevelopment. To remove them it was necessary to obtain the agreement of all the inhabitants or seek, as in most instances, an Enclosure Act from Parliament. In 1792 such an Act was obtained for Basford. This had been sought by the owners, the Duke of Newcastle, lord of the manor, Ichabod Wright and Jeffrey Brook.

Some of the earliest houses, in Hooley Place, survived until a small clearance area was declared in the 1950s.

The Act was followed by an award from enclosure commissioners, surveyors who prepared a schedule of the amounts to be reallocated to the owners and delineated new boundaries and sites for roads or streets, as set out on an enclosure map. At Basford the ancient route from Nottingham to Mansfield had already been made a turnpike road along which travellers in wheeled vehicles had to pay tolls. The award dealt with land to the west of the Mansfield Road for about a mile and the east as far as the parish boundary with the borough, the Woodborough Road. The southern part of the enclosure bordered on Radford parish and the northern part of the borough. To the north, as far as the Arnold boundary, was designated as Sherwood because of its origins in the Forest. A map of 1824 does not show Sherwood, but a part of it is described as Gloke Hill. The main owners of the newly enclosed land were the Duke of Newcastle, Henry Cavendish, Ichabod Wright and Mrs Sarah Coupe Sherbrooke.

Mansfield Street still has traces of an earlier Sherwood.

Sanderson's map of 1835 names Sherwood Place as an area on the east side of Mansfield Road extending southwards from today's Woodthorpe Drive, then known as Swine House Road. The map also shows the layout of a number of new streets southwards for about a mile, this being the original site of the new Sherwood. Opposite, on the west side of Mansfield Road, were Cavendish Vale, Loscoe Hill and Wood Ville, then only occupied by farms and single country houses.

In 1814 James Hooley bought an acre of land containing a farm, farm buildings and two cottages. As Hooley Street was the name later given to this part of Sherwood, it is doubtless that this was one of the earliest streets, as shown on the 1835 map. It was laid out after 1825 when Samuel Hall, a Nottingham lace manufacturer, bought a large part of Hooley's earlier purchase. He sold a part of the land to a group of six men who built about 20 houses.

White's Directory of 1832 describes Sherwood as

A more modern block of houses on Hall Street is distinguished by bay windows.

another populous district of newly built houses. Nearby were two older country houses, Daybrook Lodge and Woodthorpe House, occupied by Captain George Phillips and Martin Roe respectively. There was not then a public house, but there were two beer houses, which were not allowed to sell spirits, the Generous Briton and the Robin Hood. Apart from some shopkeepers the largest number of occupiers were bobbin net makers, 22, which was rather less than at Carrington. The growth of this trade is dealt with more fully in the chapter on Carrington.

Palm Cottages, although similar in style to Hooley Place, are not as old and are still there.

White's Directory of 1853 gives the names of 75 people living in Sherwood and Mapperley. Only two are described as framework knitters, but there were nine lace manufacturers. Samuel Burton and his son were one and his brother Robert was another. They both had factories, which by this time were power-driven, superseding the earlier bobbin net machines. There were also four hosiery manufacturers, including Arthur Liberty, with his brother George, a lace manufacturer. They later founded the fashionable London firm of Liberty Brothers. There were also two lace makers, who made lace in an unfinished state for the lace manufacturers. One of these was Leonard Ashworth who had seven children, one of whom, John, became a timber merchant and was mayor of Nottingham in 1908. The Revd Thomas Gascoyne of Cavendish House had a 'Classical and Mathematical Boarding establishment for young Gentlemen'. There were also shopkeepers and other tradesmen, but it is clear that Sherwood was already a place for wealthier employers to live, as 16 had an asterisk at the side of their names, indicating that they had their businesses in Nottingham.

In 1877 Sherwood, as part of Basford parish,

The tram shed, near Haydn Road, was later used for buses but is still there, used for other purposes.

Local Board, which was dissolved when the borough extension took place. *White's Directory* for 1883 shows that there were 35 buildings on Mansfield Road, Sherwood, which was differentiated from Carrington at Watcombe Road. There were only 12 as far as Haydn Road, which was the only street named as being off Mansfield Road. By 1902 not only were there more houses on this stretch, but several new streets led off to the west – Devon Drive, Percival Road, Newstead Street, Hardwick Road and Burlington Road. In addition there were Cullen's and Robinson's almshouses, a Wesleyan and a Methodist chapel and a branch of Lenton and Nottingham Co-operative Society. The newly erected tram terminus housed the recently opened service to Nottingham. This no doubt contributed to the failure of the Nottingham Suburban Railway line, which had opened in 1889, with a station at Sherwood. As this was at the top of the steep Winchester Street, the trams would have been more popular.

Sherwood had the distinction of having the first electric trams in 1902. Devon Drive Methodist church on the left has been replaced with a modern building.

became part of the borough. As it was only 50 years old, it had few problems which needed action and it continued to grow as before. The Nottingham School Board erected a new school on Haydn Road at the junction of Burton Street, no doubt named in honour of Samuel Burton and his sons, whose factory was nearby. Known as Sherwood Board School it had been started by the former Basford

Two more large buildings which were erected in the 1890s were the prison on what later became Perry Road and Bagthorpe workhouse and infirmary, which replaced the old Nottingham structures that were demolished when the Great Central line with its Victoria Station was constructed. The latter also had another station on Haydn Road, known as New Basford Station, which served the western part of Sherwood. The prison and the workhouse were separated from the

The handsome waterworks buildings have been demolished.

built-up area of Sherwood by farm land, which in 1920 became the site of Sherwood housing estate, built by Nottingham Corporation.

Council housing, with financial assistance by the Government, was the result of a Housing Act in 1919 and the Sherwood Estate was the second largest estate that the Corporation undertook to build. It was planned as a small garden city at a much lower density than the majority of working class houses in Nottingham. The road pattern was designed for local traffic only and existing trees were retained. The houses all had gardens, indoor toilets and bathrooms, with modern fireplaces and cooking arrangements. By August 1927, 1,083 houses had been built on the estate with four shops and a school.

A small part of the Sherwood estate land was sold to builders and other private housing schemes were undertaken in other parts of Sherwood in the 1919–1939 period. A welcome addition to Sherwood's amenities was the acquisition in 1921 of Woodthorpe Grange and its adjoining land. This was opened as a public park and the Grange became the headquarters of the Public Parks Department.

In 1937 another amenity was the building of the Metropole Cinema on Mansfield Road in art deco style. This was much more elegant than Sherwood's first cinema, the Kinema on Haydn Road. Both still exist but not as cinemas. Haydn Road also had a

modern factory, built in 1914, manufacturing knitwear. This had a bridge over Haydn Road to connect two sections of the factory, which was the scene of a disaster when it collapsed in 1934. On the opposite side of the road was a Corporation Water works with two attractive Flemish style buildings, which ought to have been saved from demolition.

Sherwood, despite its lack of military targets, had some damage during World War Two from

The Metropole Cinema has similar features to the demolished Adelphi Cinema at Bulwell, but it has survived as a supermarket.

enemy action. After the war some of the earliest working class houses were demolished under clearance orders. Sherwood Station, long since disused, was also demolished and the site used for the erection of two multi-storeyed blocks of flats, Woodthorpe and Winchester Courts.

Today, Sherwood is a mainly residential suburb, with only small-scale light industry. The heart of the suburb, Mansfield Road is a busy shopping centre from Haydn Road to Edwards Lane. It does have the disadvantage of being one of the main thoroughfares from the north into the city with heavy traffic.

SNEINTON

Sneinton is mentioned quite briefly in the Domesday Book where the name in the original Norman is Notintone. The manor is one of 63 in Nottinghamshire which were listed as land of the king. He had one carucate of land taxable, land for two ploughs, and 11 villagers had four ploughs. There were 12 acres of meadows and the value of the manor was £3. Unlike most of the other manors, the value in the English King Edward's time is not given. The name Nottingham is given in the Domesday Book as Snotingeham and there are other written records dating back to the ninth century which refer to names, with slight variations, beginning Snot... The 's' was subsequently dropped to give Nottingham, but why had it been dropped from Snotintone? There are few French words today which start Sn... and such as there are seem to have been borrowed from English. It is reasonable therefore to assume that the Normans found difficulty in pronouncing 'sn' words.

The Colwick tram terminus was just before the level crossing. The bridge over the road was for the Nottingham Suburb Railway. On the right is Doughill Wood.

Thomas Hammond drew this scene on Sneinton Hermitage in 1889. It shows two public houses and dwellings backing up to the roads. These were all cleared away for road widening.

It is therefore quite clear that the first syllable of Notintone is the same as that for Nottingham, and that both are derived from an Anglo-Saxon tribal leader, Snot. Why the 's' was later added back to Notintone and why it then became Snenton and

later Sneinton is not known. It is also clear from all this that Sneinton was formed as a settlement at about the same time as Nottingham. The hill on which St Stephen's church stands at Sneinton is only half a mile from St Mary's church at Nottingham, another clue perhaps to their common ancestor, whose name has come to be used in connection with midshipmen. The two communities appear to have co-existed peacefully, although the earliest mention of Sneinton in the borough records comes in 1396 when Roger Doket was accused of an affray without blood against Emmola Bishop, of Sneinton, by slapping her face in St Mary's Gate in Nottingham, for which he was fined six pence. The surname of Sneinton also occurs for five people in Nottingham in the 14th century, so there were obviously people moving from Sneinton to Nottingham and probably the other way.

Since Sneinton was part of the king's land in 1086, it seems appropriate that it should be shown in the Sherwood Forest survey of 1609. The survey lists nine separate parcels of land, the main inhabited part being described as Sneinton Towne of 30 acres. The map accompanying the survey shows a small cluster of buildings on both sides of a street, in about 500 square yards. There are three large fields and meadows, totalling about 600 acres, which are described as common to Sneinton. These are on the north-east and south of the town, adjoining it, and are called middle east field and Sneinton meadow. Although no strips are shown it is most likely that the three-field system was used. Another small close of 15 acres on the south-west of the town was occupied by a tenant. Next to it, and extending to the borough boundary, was a field of 12 acres owned by Sir Henry Pierrepont and let to a tenant, William Kinder. At the north end of the parish, on higher ground, is a drawing on the map of a beacon in a field called Sneinton Wood.

The population of Sneinton would have been about 250 people, judging from the names in the Protestation Return 1641/2 and the Hearth Tax Returns of 1664 and 1674. There do not seem to have been many large houses, judging by the number of hearths. Four was the largest number in 1664, for Henry Roose, with most of the others having only one or two. Ten years later Mr Rosse, probably the same Henry Roose, had seven hearths and several others had three.

Dr Robert Thoroton in his book *The Antiquities of Nottinghamshire* in 1676 gives a short account of the lordship of the manor, starting with William Brewer's family in the reign of King John when he was granted the lands in 1214. Thoroton then mentions Henry Pierrepont and his wife as being the owners of land in the early years of King Edward I, around 1280, without mentioning how they came into possession. He gives details of a court case in which they were accused of contravening the customs of the manor. In their defence they said that these only applied at the time of King John. The court considered that the customs which the Pierreponts were accused of contravening were set out in a document which referred to Notintone, which was a part of Nottingham on the side towards Arnold and that Sneinton had never been known as Notintone. This, wrote Thoroton, 'surely is the most evidently false of anything that pretended to be called a verdict'.

Thoroton also records that one Warreyn had been a freeholder of land at Sneinton and he had sold to a Roos, no doubt the same man mentioned in the Hearth Tax returns. This Roos then sold it to the Earl of Kingston, as the Pierreponts had been ennobled, and Thoroton said Sneinton was then in the possession of the Marquis of Dorchester, the earl's son.

In 1743 Archbishop Herring of York sent a letter to all the clergy in the diocese asking them to answer a number of questions about the parish.

Most of the buildings in this picture of 1948 have been demolished. They were at the junction of Sneinton Road and Windmill Lane.

The early 19th-century houses on Belvoir Hill were demolished, which opened up the view of Green's windmill.

This asked among other things for details of the number of families and how many were dissenters. The return for Sneinton did not answer any questions because there was no vicar at that date. There had been a church, dedicated to St Stephen since the 12th century, but in 1736 the Revd C. Scrope Berdmore was appointed vicar of St Mary's, Nottingham and also curate at Sneinton. He therefore gave no details about Sneinton, merely stating that he was the vicar of St Mary's and also of Holme Pierrepont. He no doubt delegated the work of Sneinton church to a deputy.

The population of Sneinton would not have been much higher in 1743 than in the previous century and only started to increase in the late 18th century. At the 1801 census it was only 558, which was much lower than the other parishes adjoining the

Some of the houses in the Walker Street area had been demolished before 1939 and sites left vacant. The houses in this picture had been knocked down, revealing the factory behind them.

borough. It only increased slowly for the next 20 years, reaching 1,212 in 1821. In 1832 *White's Directory* describes Sneinton as a populous eastern suburb of Nottingham which 'has partaken largely of the prosperity of that town'. The population was 3,567 in 1831, most of which had arisen during the last 10 years 'in which upwards of 400 new houses have been erected, forming several handsome streets on the Southwell Road'. These streets, the sites of which were later used for the construction of the Corporation bus depot, were mainly in the borough area with the houses at their eastern end in Sneinton. Like the other villages the new houses were in what *White's Directory* describes as the hamlets of New and Middle Sneinton, Element Hill and the Hermitage.

Salmon's map of 1861 does not extend to the other villages such as Lenton, Radford and Basford,

The houses on Bond Street, awaiting demolition after the houses and public house were acquired. Beyond can be seen some of the new houses built by small builders.

but does include Sneinton with details of its boundary, street names and details of the housing layout, many of them clearly back-to-back. The new parts were a little distant from the original village, mainly close to those stretching to the borough boundary. Element Hill, later known as Sneinton Elements, was a small separate district higher up the road to Carlton. The street names indicate their recent origin – Prince Street, Regent Street and Prince Regent Street. The plan also

Lees Hill footway gave access to the houses on the right and to Manor Street.

names in a general list, giving the occupations of each one. Forty of them are described as 'Mr' or 'gentleman', no doubt those who had made enough money to retire. There are also six clergymen, including nonconformists, one of whom was the Revd James Orange, who in 1840 published a directory and is himself described in later directories as lacemaker, publisher, secretary to the Operative Friends Society, land surveyor and iron and brass founder. Another resident was Richard Morley, a member of the textile firm of I. and R. Morley, who later became mayor of Nottingham on two occasions.

Other occupations included an organist, writer, artist, two solicitors, two excise officers and Thomas Morris, director of the Lunatic Asylum. This was the asylum for the town and county built in 1812 on land off Carlton Road, on Dakeyne Street at the bottom of the steep slope from what was then known as Windmill Hill Lane. The list also includes George Green, gentleman. This was the man whose name has become famous as a mathematician and who had worked with his father at the windmill which is a prominent landmark today. His father died in 1829 and the son went to study at Cambridge in 1833 after he had sold the windmill. He was shown as living in Dale Street, as was George Wagstaff, one of four corn millers at Sneinton. There were five maltsters but no brewers, so presumably the 13 public houses and beer houses brewed their own products.

A later edition of *White's Directory*, for 1864, indicates that the town had 11,048 inhabitants in 1861, with 2,589 houses. It also shows how the industry was changing. There was no mention of bobbin net makers, but there are five frame work

shows a continuous line of houses at the foot of the sandstone cliff adjoining the Hermitage. Some of the houses were built into the rock face.

Although the 1832 directory lists 69 bobbin net makers, this being the principal occupation as in the other newly expanded villages, it also lists 110

The renovated building on Sneinton Hollows was formerly the Old Wrestlers public house.

The turreted house on Castle Street had views over the Trent Valley and the adjoining house has decorative windows.

knitters, still pursuing a declining industry. Instead there were 15 lace makers and machine holders, three lace dressers and four hosiery manufacturers. Under the heading Saw Mills, Brownson and Birks, of Brunswick Mills, Hermitage Street, described themselves as manufacturers of all descriptions of mill bobbins, swifts, runners, quills, skewers, lignumvitae doubling rollers and more.

The increased population and the factory work called for increased provision for thirst quenching – nine maltsters, 19 inns and taverns and 20 beer houses. There are still seven public houses in Sneinton with names among those cited in 1864. A new church on the site of the old one was built in 1839 and the living was separated from that of St Mary's, although some of the pews came from that church. Other additions to the town were the National School and a police station.

In 1877 Sneinton, like the other parishes, was included in the extension of the borough boundaries. The borough surveyor, Marriott Ogle Tarbotton, prepared a map showing details of all the parishes to be included in the extension. This showed that Sneinton was mainly concentrated in the south-west part bordering on the borough, with the old village still small and some distance away from the newer parts. The area around the church and Belvoir Hill was mainly unbuilt on and provided uninterrupted views over the Trent valley and beyond. This led *White's Directory* to claim

'The old village is very romantic and contains a number of handsome villas and pleasant cottages.'

The western boundary of the parish abutted on to the newly built-up part of the Clay Field, St Ann's. Carlton Road was partly in the borough and partly in Sneinton as far as Long Hedge Lane (later Gordon Road), which became the boundary. Sneinton had expanded only as far as Dakeyne Street on the east side and as far as St Matthias Road on the opposite side. The road was named after the church, which had been erected in 1869, with a church school built in 1872. Beyond that point and north of the old village and the Hermitage was mainly farm land, together with a hilly part under Roughill Wood. There was therefore ample space for development when Sneinton became part of the borough in 1877. This development took place gradually up to 1939, with new housing stretching as far as the borough boundaries with Carlton and Colwick. Part of the latter was acquired by Nottingham for council housing in 1932 when the Bakersfield estate was built.

Part of the development in the last quarter of the 19th century included the Nottingham Suburban Railway, which branched off from the existing line to Lincoln and crossed over the northern part of Sneinton, involving the building of two bridges across Colwick Road and Sneinton Dale. The line proceeded towards Mapperley and Daybrook with a station in Sneinton, at Thorneywood. The line was not successful and closed in 1916. The two bridges were demolished in the 1960s.

Some of the unfit houses were scheduled for demolition in the early 20th century, as part of the city's Carter Gate redevelopment, where several streets extended into Sneinton. Further clearances were made in the 1930s, mainly in the parts between Manvers Street and Walker Street. Several such schemes had to be postponed in 1939 because of the war. Sneinton suffered much damage in May 1941 from an air raid. St Christopher's Church, erected in 1910, was partially wrecked. There were heavy casualties when the Nottingham Co-operative Society's bakery was hit. This was on Meadow Lane in an area stretching as far as the River Trent, which had been developed mainly for industry.

There was little development in Sneinton in the early post-1946 period, although priority was given in 1950 to the demolition of Sneinton Elements. The site was redeveloped as Chedworth Estate. In 1955 further clearance areas were declared, leading to the demolition of most of the remainder of the 19th-century housing. A cleared site on Manvers Street was used for the erection of three high-rise blocks of flats.

In 1975 the area in and around the old village was declared a conservation area and shortly afterwards the derelict Green's windmill was restored to working condition. Together with an adjoining 'hands-on' science museum, it is now a popular attraction. Considerable alterations have taken place in the road pattern in the south, with a new Manvers Street link road and the extension of Daleside Road. This saw the disappearance of one of two railway lines which ran parallel to each other. Sneinton does however possess one of the relics of the Victorian age, a level crossing.

In 1989 the City of Nottingham Planning Department produced an attractive booklet called *Buildings of Sneinton*. This features 72 buildings, with a short history of each, with maps to show their position and a photograph of each one. The scope of the booklet has been extended by including some buildings which strictly speaking were not

The statue of General William Booth, founder of the Salvation Army, stands in front of his birthplace in Notintone Place, now a museum.

really eligible, as they are outside the bounds of the original parish. It does, however, describe an area that most people think of as Sneinton today. Sneinton residents have always been proud of their identity and the Sneinton Environmental Society, with its *Sneinton Magazine*, has done much to preserve its heritage.

Today consideration is being given to plans that will transform much of the industrial sector fronting to the River Trent, which if given the go-ahead will create another New Sneinton.

STRELLEY

Strelley is a small village on the western border of the City of Nottingham. About 250 yards of the one main street is in the city itself. This arose because the city extended its boundary in the 1930s when it took part of Strelley and Bilborough, the adjoining

area, into the city. Today, despite being only half a mile from the M1 motorway and bordered by a modern by-pass road on the east, it remains a quiet village which has not changed much since Victorian times. This has been due mainly to the fact that the

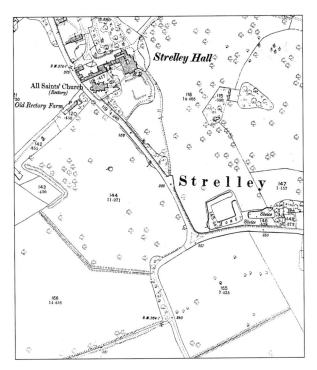

The engraving of Strelley Hall and the church was drawn by John Throsby for his 1790 additions to Dr Thoroton's *Antiquities of Nottinghamshire*.

another Nicholas Strelley managed to secure the estate, but the value of it seemed to have disappeared in lawyers' fees. This Nicholas, said Thoroton, 'lives now in Nottingham, upon some ingenious Manufactures in Glass, which he spins and orders very commendably!'

Although Dr Thoroton published his famous work in 1676 he does not mention the name of the subsequent owner of Strelley. This was Ralph Edge, who had purchased much of the estate by 1651 and completed the rest by 1682. He was the son of Walter Edge, a Staffordshire lawyer who settled in Nottingham in 1620. Ralph also became a lawyer and had a remarkable career. He became town clerk of Nottingham in 1658, was elected as an alderman and served as mayor on three occasions.

land was owned by only two families from Norman times until 1978.

Strelley had been an Anglo-Saxon settlement and in 1086 the Domesday Book records that it had only four villagers and one smallholder. It was acquired in the early years of the 12th century by a family that took its name from that of the village. Dr Thoroton traced the pedigree of the family from the time of Henry I when Walter de Stradlegh was the owner of land there. By Thoroton's time the name of both village and family had assumed its present spelling, after numerous variations. These were all derived from Old English *straet* (street) and *leah* (a clearing).

Many of the subsequent male Strelleys played important parts in local and national affairs, several of them being knighted. One of these was Sir Philip Strelley, who died in 1606. He had a son who succeeded to the estates but he, Nicholas, died without issue. The estates therefore passed through the female line but this led to disputes when Thoroton said 'This Manor hath been the inheritance of lawyers, most of my time and for some space before'. He records that eventually

This 1930s photograph of the Hall reveals some of Throsby's artistic licence.

Ralph Edge died in 1684 and his will described his extensive land ownership in Nottinghamshire and elsewhere, in addition to Strelley. He also mentioned that he had a coal-mine in Strelley, although Thoroton wrote that 'The Coals, the chief profits of Strelley are not so plentiful now as formerly!' The mines used to extract the coal were small, known as bell-pits, as the mineral was fairly close to the surface. Traces of where some of those pits had been can still be seen in fields around the village.

The Broad Oak Inn is still there but has changed since this 1930s photograph. (LSL)

Although Ralph Edge had married he had no children and the estates passed to the grandson of Richard's Aunt Catherine, who had married John Conway. As a condition of his inheritance Richard Conway changed his surname to Edge. His son, Ralph, who died in 1766, had no sons and his daughter Margaret married John Webb. Their son Thomas, on succeeding to Strelley, added Edge to his name, becoming Thomas Webb Edge (1756–1819). He had a son, with the same names, but he died unmarried in 1844. The estates then passed to his sister Mary Margaret Edge, who married James Hurt of Derbyshire. Their son James Thomas changed his surname to Edge. His son Thomas Lewis Kekewich Edge became the last male Edge to own Strelley and when he died in 1931, his daughter Emily became the owner. On her death in 1978 the estate was sold for only the second time in nearly 900 years.

The seven men who followed Ralph Edge as squires of Strelley for 250 years were typical of the landed gentry who played a prominent part in the history of rural England. Those who acquired the estates by marriage with female Strelleys were themselves possessed of their own estate on their father's decease. They all married wives from a similar background and formed a Midlands community, owning property over a wide area. They spent their time in managing their estates but were also leaders in local affairs. One of them, John Webb, served as high sheriff of Warwickshire and all the others were high sheriffs of Nottinghamshire, while the last one, T.L.K. Edge, also became an alderman on the first Nottinghamshire County Council. His daughter Miss Edge was the owner of Strelley for 47 years, dying at the age of 87 in 1978.

The Protestation Returns of 1641/2 for Nottinghamshire, which have been transcribed, usually provide some idea of the number of inhabitants of each place. Unfortunately the return for Strelley only gave the names of the minister and the parochial officers – two churchwardens, two overseers and a constable. This indicates that Strelley was a typical small village then. This is confirmed by the Hearth Tax Returns for 1664 and 1674, which have also been transcribed. In 1664 there were 20 houses for which the tax was paid. Between them the houses had 41 hearths, but the Manor House had eight and Mr William Fox had three. Not everyone paid the Hearth Tax as there was a sort of means test where those on low incomes were not charged. There were 25 of these at Strelley and all the names of the occupants are given. Thus there were 45 houses altogether, giving a population of about 200 people. The village covered about 1,800 acres and the agricultural produce would probably have been sufficient to support such a number.

Although there is no evidence that Strelley had been an open field village, cultivated in strips, it is

The public tap has not been used since 1940.

most likely that this would have been the case, like the majority of Midland Anglo-Saxon settlements. Most of these were enclosed in the 18th century, often by Act of Parliament. The pattern of small hedged fields arose from the subsequent enclosures. In 1808 an enclosure was introduced into Parliament, covering Strelley and Bilborough. The two parishes had been joined together for some time, with the Strelleys being the patrons of the living of both churches. The Act recorded that there were no open fields at Strelley as they were already enclosed. This would have been carried out by the Strelley family who, as the sole landowner, did not need an Act of Parliament to enclose.

In the first National Census of 1801 Strelley had a population of 205. *White's Directory* of 1832 describes the parish as a district of scattered dwellings containing 426 inhabitants. It goes on to add that about a mile north-west of the Hall was Strelley Park Colliery, from where coals were conveyed on a railway to the Nottingham Canal. The late 18th century had seen the beginning of what became known as the industrial revolution. The use of steam power for driving machinery, especially in the textile trades, required increased supplies of coal. The area around Strelley to the west and into Derbyshire had exposed coal measures, which although too deep for the old bell-pits could be mined with new techniques that had been developed.

In 1835 George Sanderson had published a map of 'Twenty Miles around Mansfield' based on surveys made between 1830 and 1834, at a scale of about two and a quarter miles to the inch. This is sufficient to show considerable detail, such as field boundaries. The part showing Strelley features one section less than a mile from the old village which has marked on it pits, coal pits and colliery, with a railway connecting the site to the road. This was not a railway in the sense of what later was to become a national railway with steam-driven locomotives. It would have been a track of wooden rails along which horses would pull carts. The map also shows the Nottingham Canal, opened in 1793, which flowed through adjoining parishes, with the Robbinet Arm in Strelley to the site of the pits. *White's Directory* of 1832 refers to this colliery as Strelley Park Colliery, but it was later known as Turkey Field Colliery. It had been started in 1738

Opposite the tap is the boundary marker erected in 1933 when part of the village became part of the city.

under a 99-year lease from Ralph Edge to two men, one of whom later formed the mining firm of Barber Walker. When the lease expired in 1837 it was taken over by Thomas North, a mining entrepreneur whose career is dealt with in the chapter on Cinderhill. The mine at Strelley was only a small one employing about 70 men, whereas other nearby collieries employed up to 200 men. It ceased working in the 1870s.

The more than doubling of the population from 1801 to 1831 was due to an influx of workers at the colliery. In the 20 years from 1830 to 1850 there were 70 children baptised in the parish church whose father's occupation was given as collier. They accounted for half of the children baptised in the period. Men working in collieries continued to live in Strelley after the local mine was closed, as others were sunk nearby, at Babbington and Broxtowe.

Details of the people living in Strelley in 1901 have recently become available with the release of the census enumerators' returns. The majority were engaged in agriculture and work on the estate, 35 in total, while there were 19 in mining. There were 43 occupied dwellings and some of them clearly housed people working outside the village. There was a perambulator factory manager and a lace hand, and William Oldershaw was described as chemist and druggist. His business was carried on at Long Row, Nottingham. T.L.K. Edge and his wife and five children lived at the Hall, where they had 13 servants.

T.L.K. Edge died in 1931 and in that year Nottingham City Council made a compulsory purchase

This pair of well-built houses were among the estate houses built by the Edge family.

order to acquire 591 acres of land he owned in the adjoining parishes of Bilborough and Wollaton. The following year the City Council's boundaries were extended to bring in the lands, including Bilborough, Strelley and Wollaton, where council houses were being built by the city. More land was purchased from the Edge family, including some by agreement, bringing the total acquired to nearly 1,200 acres. One estate at Bilborough was completed by 1939 but other estates were built there and on the former Strelley lands in the 1950s.

Miss Edge continued to live at Strelley Hall until she died in 1978, when the Hall and its contents were sold. The Hall was purchased for commercial use with its listed building status preserved. No further development of a substantial nature has been undertaken and today there are only about 30 houses there. The village Broad Oak Inn has been altered over the years but it has retained its original name. All Saints Church is little changed since the 15th century and has monuments to both the Strelley and Edge families.

WILFORD

In the Domesday Book Wilford appears as Wilesforde, which probably derives from Willa, an Anglo-Saxon who gave his name to the settlement on the River Trent with a ford. It seems to have been a fairly well populated place in 1086, there being 23 freemen and 13 ploughs as well as a priest, 18 acres of meadows and half a fishery. It was one of many places in the county which were given to

The charms of Wilford village, appreciated by poets and painters, were equally so by picture postcard producers. This is one of many similar scenes.

William Peverel. Like a number of nearby villages, it came under the jurisdiction of Clifton.

Dr Thoroton merely refers to it as a hamlet of Clifton, as it was not a manor. Throsby in his addition to Thoroton's book refers to it as a well-built village with an excellent parsonage.

It may seem surprising to find that Wilford is included in the Sherwood Forest survey of 1609. However, it is only the North Wilford part of the parish that is mentioned. The parish seems to have been divided into two parts, north and south of the river respectively, for many centuries, possibly as a result of the river changing its course. The North Wilford map shows the various fields, Wilford Common meadow, Wilford Pasture and Wilford Pasture park. All three were owned by Sir Gervase Clifton and there was a house on one of them.

The parish was a large one of 1,800 acres and extended as far as the boundary with West Bridgford. In the Protestation Return of 1641/2 Wilford had 81 adult men compared with West Bridgford's 99. There were 36 houses in the Hearth Tax return of 1674, about the same number as West Bridgford. Wilford had two large houses, one with eight hearths, occupied by Mr Lassels, and one with seven occupied by Mr Gervase Handley.

Two items of Wilford's history in the 18th century have been recorded and both have sombre aspects. John Deane died at the age of 82 and his tomb can still be seen in Wilford churchyard. He

had lived an adventurous life. Born in Nottingham about 1679, he turned early to crime and to avoid punishment he joined the Navy. He had a successful career, reaching the rank of captain. When he was about 30, he purchased a small ship, which he named the *Nottingham Galley*. He and his crew were able to reach a deserted island when the *Nottingham Galley* sank in a storm. They suffered to such an extent that they even contemplated killing a member of the crew to feed the rest of them.

Hunter's cottage is one of the few old houses remaining. It has recently been well renovated.

Deane eventually returned to England but then joined the Russian Navy and in 1721 was appointed British Consul in Holland. He retired in 1788 and came to live at Wilford. At the age of 61 he could be expected to live a quiet life in the village. This was not to be, as he was assaulted and robbed near his house, an offence for which the robber was subsequently hanged.

Wilford was quite close to the town of Nottingham, which it supplied with milk from the cattle which grazed in the meadows. Although there was a ford for those who wished to cross the river from South Wilford, this would only be usable in very dry weather. A ferry was normally used for the purpose, a boat which was propelled across by the ferryman hauling on a chain. In July 1784 the river was high and fast flowing and a sudden gale overturned the boat and six people including the ferryman were drowned.

The common fields were enclosed by Act of Parliament and Wilford entered the 19th century with a population of 669. In 1832 *White's Directory* was able to describe it as a delightful village with several neat villas belonging to opulent families engaged in the trade and commerce of Nottingham. These included six men described as 'Mr' or 'gent', including Mr Robert Leeson, a well-known Nottingham solicitor of the firm Jamson and Leeson. There were 12 farmers, most of whom had fairly small holdings, as well as three shoemakers, two tailors, a lace maker and a net maker.

The lane has been widened and is now a busy road. The brick buildings are the stable block of Wilford House opposite.

The directory for 1853 lists another Nottingham solicitor, William Cursham, and there are several gravestones in the churchyard belonging to this family. The number of farmers had increased to 18 and included Abraham, John, Mary and William Pyatt. John was also included as baker and miller and Mary as blacksmith.

Changes started to take place in Wilford when in September 1864 it was reported that the Wilford ferry boat had been replaced by a temporary wooden structure for foot passengers and horses until the completion of the new iron suspension bridge. This was to be built by Sir Robert Clifton but was delayed for some years. It was not completed until after he died and was opened on 16 June 1870 by his widow, Lady Clifton. It was not,

in fact, a suspension bridge but was supported on cylindrical columns. It was a toll bridge for vehicles and foot passengers and became known as the ha' penny bridge. On the same day, Lady Clifton opened another venture, on the north bank of the river, Clifton Colliery.

This was to be of some importance in 1877 when the borough announced its intention of applying for an Act of Parliament to extend its boundaries. It proposed to include the whole of the parish in the extension but this was opposed by the land owner, Henry Clifton, and the rector. The borough were more concerned to bring in the northern part because of the colliery. The proprietors had built houses for the workers and these extended as far as the borough boundary. Since the enclosure of the meadows houses had been built near to the colliery houses, so the borough was anxious to ensure that by-laws on building standards and other matters were uniform, which could only be achieved if this part of Wilford was in the borough. This was agreed by the two parties, South Wilford remaining outside the borough.

In 1894 when new district councils were set up, South Wilford became part of Basford Rural District Council. Forty years later, when county district areas were reviewed, South Wilford was included in the area of West Bridgford Urban District. This made very little difference to South Wilford as World War Two prevented any further building. Similarly after the war little change took place at first. In 1952 the inhabitants of Wilford village had to start paying rates to the City of Nottingham, the third authority in 17 years which had been the rating authority. This came about when the city was able to bring Clifton within the boundary. It was considered that the old village should also be included. The dividing line was the LNER line, which had crossed the River Trent as part of the Great Central Railway in 1900. The area to the east of the railway line remained within the area of West Bridgford Urban District and the subsequent redevelopment there is part of West Bridgford's history.

Somewhat surprisingly no one has so far written a separate history of Wilford. Robert Mellors did write a short account of some of its history in the series of *Old Nottingham Suburbs: Then and Now*. In it he wrote, in 1914, that it was 'the most painted and best illustrated village in the county'. He mentions some of the works in the Castle Museum and Art Gallery, Nottingham, which included views by Thomas Barber, John Holland Junior and a collection of 17 watercolours by Samuel W. Oscroft. Later, the picture postcard publishers contributed in no small way to our recollection of the scenes of Wilford 100 years ago. Many of these featured the old thatched cottages, most of which have been demolished. Even in 1914, Mellors wrote that many had already gone, which he did not regret, as he said most of them were insanitary, with common brick floors, very damp and without proper sinks or drains.

The lack of a written history of Wilford is perhaps due to the enthusiasm with which Nottingham's Victorian writers described it in poetry or at least verse. Foremost of these, an acknowledged gifted poet, was Henry Kirke White, who lived in

The picturesque hump-backed bridge crossed the Fairham Brook near the River Trent and led to Clifton Grove.

Wilford for a short part of his 22 years. Of the church-yard, he wrote:

'Here would I wish to sleep. This is the spot
Which I have long marked out to lay my bones in'

Another poet, Spencer T. Hall, could even find inspiration when Wilford was suffering from one of its frequent floods:

'Wilford! When first I gazed on thee.
Whilst leaning o'er upland stile.
Thy flooded meads were one vast lake.
And thou a little bowery isle.'

The residents of Wilford would not have been impressed by this in 1875 when one of the worst

Wilford House's stable block in 1964 was used for car maintenance and MOT testing.

floods of the century occurred, washing away some of the cottages with water 18ft deep. A rather less serious note to floods happened later when Judge Masterman came to live in the village. He complained to neighbours that his hens had been drowned, to which they replied 'ah well, you see, your Honour, people in Wilford keep ducks not hens'. Eventually a high bank, named the Bee bank, was built between the river and the village.

The church of St Wilfrid has a 14th-century nave, with aisles rebuilt in 1890. A stained glass window to the memory of Henry Kirke White has a marble medallion bust of him. There are other monuments in the church including those to Henry Smith and his wife Lady Lucy, a daughter of the Earl of Leven and Melville. They lived in the house

at the south end of the village known as Wilford House. This was built in 1781 for Samuel Smith, a member of the banking family, of which the founder formed the first English provincial bank in Nottingham. The house was later sold in the late 19th century to T. Bailey Forman, proprietor of Nottingham newspapers. The house was then used as living accommodation for employees of the newspaper group before being skilfully restored and becoming a listed building. On the opposite side of Clifton Lane is another listed building, the former stable block of Wilford House. The adjoining land was used as a garden centre but is now occupied by recently built houses and a public house.

Wilford toll bridge and toll house in 1971 before the bridge was replaced by a footbridge. The toll house remains.

Main Road runs from the Wilford Lane crossroads northwards and although most of the houses in the village are of the 20th century there are a number of older buildings, eight of which are on the list of buildings of special interest. A telephone box is also on the list. Hunter's Farm has the date 1724 pricked out in brickwork on a gable end, while the former infants' school has the date 1828 above the door. The Endowed School, built in 1736 by the Revd Benjamin Carter, was rebuilt in 1886 and has recently been extended. A little further on are the Dorothy Boot Homes built by Sir Jesse Boot (later Baron Trent) in 1908 for veterans of the Crimean and Indian mutiny campaigns. At the end of the village is a small green with trees, which stand in front of a row of glebe cottages.

The gazebo or summerhouse in the north-west corner of the churchyard also served as a mortuary for bodies drowned in the river.

Adjoining the church is the 18th-century rectory with outbuildings, while in the north-west corner of the churchyard is a summer house or gazebo, the lower part of which was used from time to time as a mortuary for persons drowned in the river.

Beyond are sports grounds leading to the renewed Wilford Bridge, which replaced the former toll bridge. After the City Council incorporated Wilford, it was able to buy the bridge and discontinue the tolls. The new bridge is for pedestrians and cyclists only, so there is no through traffic, which helps to retain something of the village atmosphere.

Across the river, in North Wilford, the same cannot be said. This part of the area has seen considerable changes since 1870 when the colliery was built. In the 1920s an electricity generating station was erected on an adjoining site, as part of the national grid. This coal-fired station was considerably enlarged in the years immediately after World War Two, but apart from pylons and switch-gear nothing remains of it. The colliery too has gone and the whole area has been developed with a large retail and industrial park. The road in front is an extension of Queen's Drive in the Meadows and is a busy road feeding Clifton Bridge and Lenton Lane.

WOLLATON

Wollaton has been part of the City of Nottingham for only 70 years. In the Domesday Book the main manor was one of the many holdings of William Peverel. Written, presumably phonetically by a Norman who did not recognise 'w', as Olavestone, it had a tenant, Young Wulfsi, while Warner William's man had one plough and seven freemen, and four villages had four ploughs. There was also underwood one league long and one furlong wide. It had fallen in value from 100 shillings before 1066, to 60 shillings. In addition, as part of the land of the king there was one carucate of land for one plough. Describing the land as an outlier and waste, the scribe must have been more familiar with English as he called it Waletone.

There was also an entry under the lands of the king's thanes, who held land by special grant. This was named Sutone, (Sutton) which later had Passeys added to it. This was stated to have jurisdiction in Olavestone (Wollaton). Wherever it was is not now known, as it is a 'lost village', only remembered today by Sutton Passeys Crescent. The name came from a tenant Robert le Passeis, while Wollaton was 'Wulflafs farm'.

Dr Thoroton traced the descendants of Warner, William's man, down to the reign of King Henry I, who died in 1135. The next owner of Wollaton was Robert Mortein and six generations later William Mortein died without a male heir. His sister Isabella married Richard Willoughby, whose father, also Richard, had acquired most of the Wollaton land from William Mortein.

The Willoughby family retained Wollaton until 1923 when it was sold to Nottingham Corporation. The family had taken its surname from the village

'Lovely art thou fair Wollaton; magnificent are thy features!' enthused John Throsby in his poetic description to accompany this engraving of the Hall in 1790.

of Willoughby-on-the-Wolds after Richard Bugge changed it. His father had been a merchant of Nottingham and Richard apparently disliked the surname Bugge as it was used as a term for hobgoblin or spectre (later used as a name for an insect and concealed listening device).

The old pump with its shelter forms a central feature in the heart of the old village.

The Willoughbys had as their armorial bearings water bougets (pronounced 'booge') as they were already a family of some standing and, as Thoroton put it, 'the original ancestors of diverse good families'. Their Willoughby descendants, of whom Thoroton traced 12 generations, were even more illustrious. The Sir Richard who married Isabella Mortein became a judge and even Chief Justice when the holder of that office was abroad. Another member, Sir Hugh, led an expedition to discover new lands in 1554 but he and his crew were frozen to death in the Arctic after a storm.

Possibly the most notable of the Willoughby line was Sir Francis, who died in 1596. He had started to build a new house for the family in parkland adjoining the village. It took eight years to finish and was financed by exchanging coal from the nearby pits for Ancaster stone from Lincolnshire.

The coal was transported on one of England's first railways, drawn of course by horse-wagons. Described as one of the most important Elizabethan mansions in England, it was designed in part by Sir Francis himself, especially some of the more extravagant features. However, much of the design was by Robert Smythson, who already had designed a similar house at Longleat.

The Admiral Rodney hotel is one of a group of buildings that surround the square.

The building of the Hall almost ruined Sir Francis financially and matters were not improved after his death. He had no male heir by his first wife and married as his second wife a much younger lady in the hope of a male heir. She only managed to produce a daughter, after strict precautions were taken to prevent the substitution of the girl, by a clandestine plot, with a boy. The mother later caused a great deal of the estate's wealth to vanish, to try to claim the estate. This however went to Sir Percival Willoughby, who had married a daughter of Sir Francis. Sir Percival was a member of another Willoughby family, from Eresby in Lincolnshire.

Sir Percival's grandson Francis became a distinguished naturalist, touring the Continent collecting specimens and making notes describing them. His eldest son was made a baronet but died unmarried, the baronetcy passing to his brother, who was created a peer as Lord Middleton in 1711, the title being that of the Willoughby's estate in Warwickshire. His son married an heiress of Birdsall, Yorkshire, and subsequent members made their main residences at the other two houses, Wollaton being occasionally let to tenants.

Wollaton in the 18th century would be little changed from early years as a quiet agricultural village. The presence of the coal mines did make some difference as is a letter from the mayor of Nottingham dated 25 August 1756 reveals. The letter, addressed to the Secretary of State, said that a great number of colliers and other persons entered the town armed with stakes, hatchets and pick-axes, shouting and making a great noise. The Riot Act was read and three men were seized and imprisoned. The men were from Cossall and Trowell and were employed to work Lord Middleton's coal pits at Wollaton. They were protesting about the price of corn but they were released when the crowd agreed to disperse. The letter was sent by the mayor of Nottingham to warn the government that it might be necessary for the military to be sent for.

John Throsby, who in 1796 updated Thoroton's book, described Wollaton as small with 50 dwellings and said that it 'abounds in coal'. In 1801 the population of the village was 838, only slightly less than the adjoining Lenton. The coal mines and the maintenance of the Willoughby estate and park would provide employment in addition to that on farms. By the census of 1851 the population had fallen to 681 in 118 houses. The occupations of the male adults were mainly either coal miners or agricultural labourers, together with a few other trades such as joiners, bricklayers and shopkeepers. Mrs Neville Webb-Edge appears to have been the tenant at the Hall. She was a widow aged 50 with six servants and no doubt had been married to a member of the Edge family of Strelley.

The rector, the Revd Charles Willoughby, aged 29, had five children aged four and under but his wife had five servants to help her. There were four farmers who, apart from the rector and the parish clerk, were the only men occupying land, which enabled them to vote for Members of Parliament.

Opposite St Leonard's Church is the brick house, with a string course and gothic windows, next to a stone-built house.

By 1901 the population had fallen to 541 but the 1902 *Wright's Directory* stated that the coal mine, now owned by a limited company, had 1,200 hands, producing 1,800 tons of coal each day. Most of those would live in nearby Radford and other parts of the city. In 1920 the Corporation of Nottingham sought an extension of its boundaries, including taking in Wollaton. A representative of the miners union gave evidence that many of them lived outside Wollaton. Some 600 arrived at work each day at Radford railway station as one shaft of Wollaton started there. They came from as far away as Bulwell, from where one man had walked both ways every day for 40 years and another man walked from Kimberley. The union supported the proposed extension as it would enable the City Council to build houses at Wollaton if it succeeded. It did not succeed but four years later the Corporation purchased Wollaton Hall and the whole of the estate, part of which was in fact already part of the city. The council proceeded to erect houses on the northern part of the estate adjoining the park but these were not generally for miners. The housing scheme was an innovative one, built partly on land in the city and partly in Basford Rural District. The estate was situated on both sides of a 120ft-wide new road, Middleton Boulevard, part of a planned route to by-pass the city. The council had a waiting list for council houses and sought to find a speedier way of building. It decided on a type named 'Crane' bungalows, after the chairman of the Housing Committee. The construction used light steel stancheons and roof trusses with walls of concrete and plaster slabs. They were erected by skilled members of engineering trades and unskilled labourers, and this enabled rapid completion. Later some brick houses were also built, and 813 dwellings were completed by 1928. A novel feature of this scheme, and one never repeated by the council, was to offer them for sale, with weekly payments for 20 years, at an amount several shillings a week more than rent. Not everyone could afford such an amount, but just under a half were sold.

Part of undeveloped Wollaton bordering Bilborough was acquired for erecting council houses in the 1930s and other privately owned houses were built on both sides of Wollaton Road. After World War Two more houses, both council and private, were built on the west side of the parish, which in 1932 came wholly within the city. In the 1960s a part of Balloon Woods, on the north-west corner of Wollaton, was used for the erection of a large estate using a non-traditional method of construction. This included low-rise flats with walk-ways at first floor level. The scheme proved to be a failure mainly due to construction faults and the whole was demolished within 20 years. The site has been redeveloped with traditional houses.

Today Wollaton is almost entirely residential, the colliery having been closed in the 1950s. Wollaton Hall and park are one of Nottingham's finest assets, the Hall at present housing a natural history museum, while an industrial museum has been sited in the adjoining former stable block. The lake and herds of deer are a reminder of the mediaeval foundation of the estate. The grounds have been used for a variety of purposes, ranging from agricultural shows, pageants, and car rallies to pop concerts. Part of the land is a private golf course.

The heart of the old village retains much of its

To the west of the pump is the row of 18th-century cottages on Bramcote Lane.

rural appearance with its square and village pump with shelter. There are several older houses, which are listed buildings. The part around the village is a conservation area and the church of St Leonard is a Grade I listed building.

Forty years after the Wollaton Park estate was built came the sharp contrast of Balloon Woods, admittedly only just within the parish boundary. Sighs of relief must have been heard when its demolition was announced.

Much of the church is late 14th century or earlier and it contains a number of monuments to members of the Willoughby family and their successors. A square inscription records the contribution of Robert Smythson to the building of the Hall, describing him as 'architector and surveyor'.

The residents of Wollaton are proud of their heritage and have formed a society to ensure its future.

PART TWO:
THE OUTER SUBURBS

ARNOLD

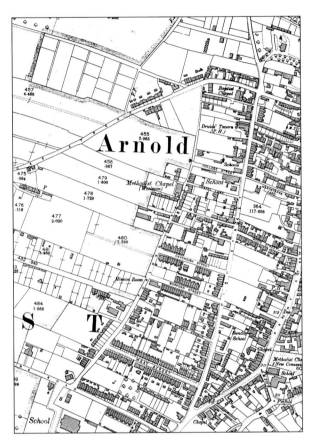

The photographer of this picture postcard no doubt considered this street to be the principal street of the town, although there was no Main Street. As it appears to descend at the end of the picture, it was probably the steep road from the road to Woodborough, Coppice Road. (LSL)

Ernehale, as Arnold is referred to in the Domesday Book, is thought to mean 'eagle's nook or corner'. From the 13th century onwards the initial letter always appears as 'A', with the suffix '-old' appearing by the 15th century. The land was held by William Peverel and the Domesday Book entry is rather more informative than usual. The last English King Edward had three carucates of land taxable. There was land for 11 ploughs with 20 villagers and four small-holders. Further information is that there was woodland pasture in various places, three leagues long and three wide. Ernehale's value had increased from £4 and two

sesters of honey before 1066 to £8 and six sesters of honey. The measurement of three leagues long and three wide is puzzling as all maps from 1609 onwards show Arnold as a long narrow parish. Three leagues would be about four and a half miles, which agrees with the length given in subsequent records. Perhaps the width of three leagues included lands in adjoining parishes.

Arnold was part of Sherwood Forest and the village seems to have developed alongside a track northwards in a valley, as the lands to the east rose steeply to Mapperley and Woodborough. The Sherwood Forest survey map of 1609 shows the 'Towne of Arnhall' stretching for about two-thirds of a mile either side of the track. There appear to be about 75 dwellings, most of them with land behind them of up to 500ft. The survey itself gives details of 49 separate holdings. The largest, of 1,721 acres, covers the whole of the northern part of the parish and is common to the whole of Arnhall, including some woods. Other large common fields covering 1,598 acres included one of 242 acres, Common Wood. The names of freeholders

The two main streets, Front Street and High Street, ran parallel to each other with small streets and yards connecting them. Arthur Packer is not included in a directory for 1899, but in the 1904 edition he is described as grocer, 48 Front Street. Hopewell is not in either directory but John Hopewell, clothier, Front Street, is in the 1907 edition. (LSL)

include the king, Lady Markham and Thomas Cludd, together with five other smaller ones. Including tenants the names given amount to 16, while there are a number of smallholdings of less than an acre without tenants' names. The village can thus be seen as quite large compared with others, with a good deal of common land and woodlands.

The Protestation Return of 1641/2 lists 114 names of men over the age of 18. There were 80 separate surnames, because some adult sons would register as well as fathers. This would indicate that there would probably be about 350 total population. The Hearth Tax Return of 1674 shows that there were at least 60 houses, there being that number paying the tax while those too poor to be assessed are not necessarily listed. A Mr Chadwick had the largest number of hearths, seven, and Mr Crosse had five.

Dr Thoroton in his book published in 1676 mentions a number of men who had manors in

Arnold from time to time, starting with Richard who took the name de Arnhall as his surname in about 1175. The manor ownerships changed hands frequently and some of the owners include the Nevill family, the Earl of Hereford, John Merbury, Sir Thomas Rempston, Sir William Hastings, William Stanhope and Samuel Cludd, Thomas being mentioned in the 1609 survey.

When Archbishop Herring called for an account of each parish in 1743, there were 120 families in Arnold including 18 Presbyterians. The vicar had some hard things to say about the schoolmaster who was also the clerk of the meeting house (nonconformist), although the school belonged to the church. He 'takes no care to instruct the children in the principles of the Church of England nor does he care to bring them to church and very rarely comes himself.' He also complained that the master would not leave the schoolhouse, to which he was not entitled. The vicar concluded that the

Andrew Carnegie was born in Scotland but his family emigrated to America when he was 13. He founded the largest iron and steel works and died a multi-millionaire. He used £70,000,000 of his fortune to found various institutions in Britain and America. His library was designed by an Arnold architect, W.H. Higginbotham, and opened in 1906. (LSL)

master was 'a very illiterate man and in my opinion by no means a proper person for a schoolmaster.'

An enclosure Act was obtained in 1789, the petitioners being William Coape Sherbrooke, John Need, Robert Padley, Edward Jones and other lords of manor. The award covered 2,848 acres, over half the parish. John Throsby, in his addition to Dr Thoroton's account, said that Arnold extended endways for three miles into the forest and was mostly good land. 'The village is near a mile in length and in it are many new buildings.' He added that cotton-mills had been erected on a large scale by Dawson (in fact Davison) and Hawksley and there was a worsted mill which employed 50 children.

The growth in population since 1743 is shown by the first National Census in 1801, when it was 2,768. Arnold was also a village of home-based stocking frames as well as the mills. This was a declining industry by the beginning of the 19th century and in 1811 the Luddite riots and frame-breaking were a serious threat. The Luddites were well organised and around Nottingham had four separate gangs, one of which was at Arnold. In March 1811, 63 frames, chiefly belonging to Messrs Bolton, were destroyed in one night.

The cotton and worsted mills could not compete with Lancashire and closed, leaving Arnold mainly dependent on the stocking frames. William Felkin,

the author of the standard history of lace and hosiery, published in 1867, conducted a census of the number of stocking frames in and around Nottingham in 1844. After the borough itself, which held 3,490, the next highest number was 1,397 at Arnold. This was a high proportion as the population had only grown to 4,704 in 1851, that is less than doubled. Compare this with Basford, which increased five-fold in the same period. Arnold was still mainly producing hosiery and gloves on the frames, whereas the other districts were producing lace.

Arnot Hill House and grounds were acquired by the Urban District Council just before World War One, but before they could use them a war-time contingent of the British Red Cross occupied it. The House later became the headquarters of the Urban District Council. (LSL)

White's Directory for 1853 lists only two lace manufacturers, compared with 29 hosiery agents, eight framesmiths and three sinker makers. On the other hand there were 30 farmers and five cow-keepers and the northern half of the parish was largely agricultural and woodland. The directory gives the names of 57 of the principal inhabitants, of whom 13 lived at Redhill and one at Daybrook. Redhill had developed as a hamlet mainly due to its position on the road to Mansfield and Ollerton. The road to Mansfield had been turnpiked in 1787.

The lack of prosperity due to the decline in the stocking-frame industry meant that living conditions in the mid-19th century were poor. Although an Act of Parliament of 1848 granted districts such as

Arnold the right to appoint a Local Board of Health, at least some of the inhabitants were reluctant to do so. A scathing report to the Government's General Board of Health listed some of the deficiencies. Houses were badly roofed, some being alleged to have been built by squatters, and inadequate drainage and sewers and contaminated water supplies were among the defects. One spring, which was used by a group of dwellings, was also used by cattle. Pigs were often housed close to dwellings and of course all these factors meant infectious diseases spread rapidly. A proposal in 1854 to set up a Board was opposed by some of the wealthier inhabitants who would have had to bear most of the expense through rates. However, as all the inhabitants were allowed to say whether they wanted a Board or not and most of the working population supported the idea, a Board was formed in 1854.

In 1859 William Stumbles gave a talk in the General Baptist Chapel to a 'Young Mens' Improvement Society' on Arnold's history of the previous 100 years. He prefaced his remarks by saying 'there is nothing in the national or historical character of the village that furnishes matter for elaborate description'. He also commented that there were some sad features in social conditions and morals of the poor. There was Sabbath-breaking, drunkenness, few marriages and a large proportion of illegitimate children. This was in spite of the existence of nonconformist chapels of Wesleyans, Kilhamites, Primitive Methodists, General and Particular Baptists, as well as a growing concern on the part of the parish church incumbents.

There were, however, others who tried to provide for a better way of life, in a manner rather ahead of its time. One of these was the Arnold

The charabanc was a favoured vehicle for outings in the 1920s and the ladies in this one would have had their hats held in place by hat pins for when the charabanc reached its top speed of anything up to 20mph. The canopy at the rear kept the rain off when pulled forward.

The road northwards through Redhill was in a ravine and the bridge was built to allow communication between the few farms on either side. (LSL)

gradually expanded, especially when the Great Northern Railway opened the Nottingham to Pinxton line with a station there. The Nottingham Suburban Railway, started in 1889, also used the station. In 1879 the horse bus service went to Nottingham seven times a day.

Another source of employment was the sinking of Bestwood Colliery, which was near enough for Arnold men to travel to, as well as Gedling Colliery from 1902. Public improvements included British and National Schools, Offices for the Local Board with a fire engine house and a weighing room, a free library and a working men's institute. By 1883 there were six Odd Fellows lodges, five Benefit Societies and a Cottage Garden Society.

Between 1881 and 1901 the population increased from 5,745 (only just double the figure for 1801) to 8,757. The building of houses led to the creation of a new parish, Daybrook with part of Carrington, and the erection of St Paul's Church in 1898. The period from 1901 to 1914 saw another substantial increase in population to 11,147 in 1911. The Edwardian era also saw the coming of the Nottingham Corporation Trams to Arnold, and this perhaps encouraged the creation of a new suburb, clearly separated at first from Daybrook. This was the area from Thackerays Lane to the boundary with the city on Woodthorpe Drive. The houses were all designed for high earners such as professionals and businessmen. *Kelly's Directory* for 1916 lists, as usual, a separate list of private residents of 100 men, 80% of whom lived in the new suburb which extended to Mapperley Plains at Woodthorpe. A similar list in the 1904 edition contained only 50 names and this was before the Woodthorpe Estate had been started.

The estate was to be a bone of contention in 1920 when a Ministry of Health enquiry looked into the city's application for a boundary extension.

Community Society, a self-help body whose aims were to provide support to its members in time of sickness and with a comfortable life in old age. Members paid 1s a month (females sixpence) and if sick received a weekly payment of at least 6s. The rules and regulations were printed and it sets out procedures that were later laid down under the National Insurance scheme. Conduct of meetings was also subject to the rules, one of which stated that if any member spoke without rising to his feet, he was to be fined one penny.

The last quarter of a century saw an improvement generally in Arnold. The work of the Local Board, which included submission of plans for new buildings, was carried on from 1896 by the newly formed Urban District Council. New industries were started, one of them being the transfer in 1877 of Allen Solly's hosiery concern from Godalming, employing 500 people. *Morris's Directory* of 1879 includes a branch of the Nottingham hosiery firm I. and R. Morley, as well as several other hosiery firms. Daybrook Laundry was established then, as were a branch of the Lenton and Nottingham Co-operative Stores and Arnold Co-operative Manufacturing Company. John Robinson had a maltster's business and was later to start the Home Brewery at Daybrook. This former hamlet to the south of the parish had

The farm was attached to the Guide House on Redhill, an ancient dwelling where travellers could obtain information or even a guide through the sparsely populated Sherwood Forest. John Gadsby junior, a farmer at Redhill, is mentioned in a 1904 directory. (LSL)

The city proposed to bring Arnold and the other urban districts into its jurisdiction. Much was made by counsel for the city of the fact that the Woodthorpe estate on the city boundary was in reality a part of the city, with most of its inhabitants earning a living there. The proposal was rejected by the Minister of Health.

Arnold in 1920 had a diversified industrial base with the three large textile factories, the brewery, the laundry, and the two nearby collieries, all employing large numbers of workers. A variety of local shops and services all contributed to its self-sufficiency. 1920 also saw two important developments, the use of the former Arnot Hill House for the Urban District Council and the start of council house building. With the help of financial subsidies both the Urban District Council and private builders were able to build new, more modern homes, the latter mainly being for sale to owner-occupiers. The district was to increase in population more or less continuously from then

onwards, apart from during World War Two. After the war a start was made in demolishing the older unfit houses in the heart of the old village. This enabled the pedestrianisation of the centre and building as far as the east, west and south borders of the district. Some building took place northwards but stopped short of the northern boundary, leaving a large area of undeveloped land.

The character of Arnold has changed in the last 30 or so years, due to several factors which affected Arnold more so than many other places. The closing of the railway line, the decline in the manufacturing textile industries, the closing of the two collieries and the loss of the brewery and the laundry all combined to reduce local employment opportunities. These have been replaced in some degree by newer industries such as light industry, services and retail outlets. To a greater extent than ever before people now have to travel to work, especially to the city. The latter too has seen the flight of major manufacturing industries but has

William Herbert Higginbotham was an architect with an office in Bridlesmith Gate, Nottingham, but he lived in Front Street, Arnold. He had been an Urban District Councillor. (LSL)

been able to replace them with leisure, educational and services such as finance.

The absorption of the Urban District Council in 1974 into Gedling Borough Council has helped to create a new Arnold of growing importance to the nearby mainly rural areas. Arnold's population today is approaching 40,000 and its 15,000 or so houses are mainly less than 40 years old. On the map it appears as part of a built-up area joined to Nottingham and Carlton, but having survived several attempts by the city to enlarge its boundaries, Arnold has retained its own individual character.

ATTENBOROUGH

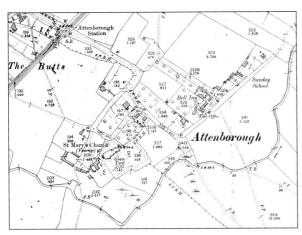

There is no mention of Attenborough in the Domesday Book although its name, originally 'Adda's burh', refers to an Anglo-Saxon foundation. The Domesday Book refers to both Toton and Chilwell, each of which had the right to half a church. So, as Dr Thoroton was to describe it, Attenborough (which for once he spelled the same as its modern name) 'is rather to be called a church than a village, having but few houses and no fields'. However Attenborough, as it had a church, was a parish whereas Toton and Chilwell were not.

The attendant at Nottingham Castle Museum is seen here holding a mammoth's tusk found when excavations took place in around 1931. (LSL)

121

The reason for this may lie in the geology of the area. Attenborough was built on a deep gravel bed adjacent to the River Trent and it may be that in the Neolithic age a settlement was there on a small island which was slightly higher than the land round about, which could be expected to flood in winter leaving the island untouched. Recent excavations at Gamston a few miles downstream revealed that a similar settlement had been there in the Iron Age, with a similar explanation.

The church of St Mary Magdalene dates back to the early 13th century, although there was perhaps a church there in 1086, as the Domesday Book mentions one. Its splendid spire is a notable landmark in the flat Trent Valley. This drawing from the east is dated 1867. (LSL)

The present church has architecture of the 13th century but is probable that there had been an earlier, perhaps Anglo-Saxon one. What is certain is that there had been Neolithic habitation. The gravel beds, because of their drainage and depth, have helped to preserve artefacts from that period as well as animal remains. There are later written records of the church as it was granted by its Norman overlord partly to Lenton Priory and partly to the Grey family of Codnor. A list of rectors dates back to 1230.

The somewhat anomalous parish situation is not made much clearer by the Protestation Return of 1641/2, which was compiled parish by parish. Under Attenborough were 42 names of men over 16, in place of the more usual 18. These included four men described as overseer and churchwarden

in each case. In addition Richard Barker, Thomas Stanfielde and Richard Wright were described as constables of Toton, Chilwell and Bramcote. Gervase Dodson was the vicar and a note added that he, with others, was indicted in 1631 for riotous affray. There were also separate lists of names for Bramcote, Chilwell and Toton, which shared the same minister and the other offices.

The Hearth Tax Return of 1674 is similarly not very helpful. One list for Attenborough, headed 'part of Attenborough' had four names with a total of six hearths, three of which were Mrs Standish's. Another list for Toton and Attenborough gives 20 names liable for tax plus another nine who were not chargeable. There were 40 hearths, of which seven were owned by Mr John Foulgham and six by Arthur Warin Esq.

This photograph of the early 1900s was taken from the north-west. It shows the house near the church, which is reputed to have been the home of the Cromwellian General Henry Ireton. (LSL)

It is known that there was at least one farmhouse to the west of the church because it was recorded that Henry Ireton was born there in 1611. He became a general in the Parliamentary army in the Civil War and later married Cromwell's daughter Bridget. He was one of those who signed the King's death warrant. He died in 1651 before the restoration of the monarchy and was buried in Henry VII's chapel in Westminster Abbey. After the Restoration his body was removed and hanged from the Tyburn gallows.

In 1839 the Midland Railway line from Nottingham to Derby was opened with a station at Attenborough. It was hardly likely to be of much use to the village at that time but was to become so during World War One when it became the nearest station to the munitions factory at Chilwell. Today the frequent trains to Derby and to London pass through, keeping the level-crossing keeper busy as well as annoying motorists. In 1879 *Morris's Directory* could record only two gentry, Mr James Bradbury of Orchard House and Mr Edwin Morley. The trades and professions only ran to four people, a shopkeeper, a farmer, a cottager and the landlord of the Bell Inn who was also the parish clerk.

The Midland Railway separates the village part of Attenborough from the rest, which has been developed in recent years. This house is one of the earlier houses of which there are only about 20, built in 1901.

In the 1901 census returns the population of 161 people lived in 42 houses. Eight of the heads of households were manufacturers of textiles, and there were also a county clerk, two architects, a traveller, the stationmaster and a teacher. Most of these were working elsewhere, mainly in Nottingham. The rest of the heads were mainly manual workers and farm labourers.

Between the railway line and the River Trent lie the lagoons left behind when extraction of gravel commenced in the 1920s. They have been developed into an extensive managed nature reserve, noted particularly as a winter residence for migratory wildfowl.

An important change in the 1920s was the start of excavation of gravel in the area between the railway lines by Trent Gravels Limited. This was to continue for many years and residents in the early years were dismayed to find that the gravel was not replaced by soil. Instead the large holes were allowed to fill with water to form lagoons. Today, however, these have been made into what Attenborough is perhaps best known for, the nature reserve, with proper management.

Development of the village west of the railway line has taken place following the major road alterations in the post-1945 era with new houses, which are indistinguishable from similar ones in adjoining Chilwell and Toton. The village itself still retains its rural atmosphere and a strong sense of community prevails among the residents. A publication, *20th Century Attenborough*, was published in 2000 and consists entirely of contributions from residents, which reveal the varied activities and organisations of the village. The neatly produced booklet credits neither author nor publisher but its 76 pages cover 35 different aspects of life there today. There is a copy in Nottingham Local Studies Library and no doubt there are others in libraries in the Beeston area.

BEESTON

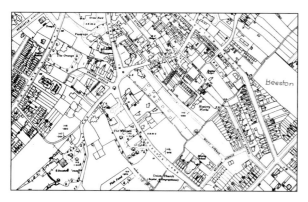

Beeston is one of a number of Anglo-Saxon settlements along the River Trent. It was not until the late 19th century that archeological excavations revealed that man had lived in the area in the Neolithic and Bronze Age eras. The entry in the Domesday Book is uncomplicated. Part of William Peverel's extensive manors, three Anglo-Saxons had three carucates of land. There was land for four ploughs, William having in lordship two ploughs, while 17 villagers and one freeman had nine ploughs. There were 24 acres of meadow and the value before 1066 and after was unchanged at 30s. The site of the Anglo-Saxon settlement was about one mile from the River Trent and the prefix to its name probably derives from 'beosuc', meaning 'bent grass', which grew in the fields.

The earliest lords of the manor that Dr R. Thoroton could find were the Bellocampo family in the early 13th century. The family is mentioned by him several times down to 1348, sometimes in the Latin and sometimes as the French Beauchamp. He also mentions that Poultrells and Willoughby had land there. After the dissolution of the monasteries he mentions several subsequent owners, concluding that some land came into the Charlton family, who retained it until the 20th century. The last lords of the manor from Elizabethan times were the Strey family who lived at the manor house, which was later incorporated into the house that is still there today.

The Protestation Return of 1641/2 lists 91 names of adult men, but the reliability seems suspect as there seems to be duplication in several cases and 'Thomas Lacie' appears three times. Henry and Robert Smalley are both described as 'Church Mester'. Is this an example of Nottinghamshire vernacular? The Hearth Tax Return of 1674 seems more reliable, although it lists a Mr Mary West. It

Although described as The Cross, the only structures are lamp-posts. The Cross used to stand here but disappeared many years ago. Part of the steps and shaft were discovered after this picture was taken and can be seen near the old school by the parish church. (LSL)

indicates that there 60 dwellings, three of which had each six hearths.

Although Beeston had been open field like many other Midland villages, an early 17th-century lawsuit revealed that there had been some enclosure already. A Parliamentary Enclosure Act was not obtained until 1806, which only affected 822 acres.

Beeston started to change in the 18th century, when two main roads through the village were turnpiked, and later when the Beeston Canal was cut. Like other villages around Nottingham it became a semi-industrial village when the stocking

The photograph is dated 1929. In a 1920 directory Percy Hickling was a motor and general engineer, Central Garage, 85 High Road, and Benjamin Kirk was the licencee of the Durham Ox public house, 83 High Road. (LSL)

frame industry grew. At the first census of 1801 it had a population of 948, which had increased to 2,530 in 1831, when there were 42 bobbin net makers with over 100 machines, or stocking frames. Five years later a census of bobbin net machines gave the figure for Beeston as 69. There was also an early factory at Beeston. William Lowe's silk mill was built in 1826. It burned down at the same time as Nottingham Castle but was rebuilt in the 1840s and was to employ about 580 people by 1851, out of a population of 3,016. Part of the building still remains.

Another important event in 1839 was the construction of the railway line from Nottingham to Derby, with a station at Beeston. This effectively divided Beeston into two halves with an inconvenient level crossing, which was replaced by a bridge in 1939. The railway no doubt helped Beeston to develop considerably in the second half of the 19th century. In 1853 it was still partly agricultural and partly industrial. The industry, apart from the silk mill, was mainly small scale. There were still eight framework knitters and five frame-smiths, together with 22 fancy net makers. On the other hand there were 14 farmers. The population increased only slowly for the next 20 years, adding a mere 118 to the number of residents, but there was a jump of 1,300 between 1871 and 1881.

In 1871 the increasing urbanisation was recognised by the formation of a Local Board. A school board was set up in 1880 and a growing trend for home ownership was reflected by the establishment of the Mutual Permanent Benefit Building Society with 300 members.

The textile industry was becoming increasingly housed in power-driven factories, starting in 1871 with the tall Anglo-Scotia mills on Wollaton Road, where Wilkinson and Company made lace curtains and Shetland shawls. Another factory, Pollard's, had 11 tenants as machine holders. Foster and Pearson's, iron founders, later became one of the

The tall building in the centre of this picture is the old silk mill rebuilt after the 1831 riots, part of which is still standing. On the left is the sunblind of Farrands, 40 High Road, one of the multiple shops of Frank Farrands Limited, grocers. A few doors away can be seen the shop with the ubiquitous façade of one of F.W. Woolworth and Company Limited's shops. This appears in a 1936 directory, which helps to date the picture to the late 1930s, confirmed by the car opposite. (LSL)

town's links with horticulture as builders of greenhouses. Other new industries were started in the last decades and this diversification was to be a continuing feature of Beeston. These included the Humber Cycle Works, the Beeston Foundry Company, which later changed its name to the Beeston Boiler Company, and Beeston Brewery, which introduced a pneumatic process of malting. Another industry new to the area was creosote dipping of railway sleepers.

The increase in population from 1881 to 1901 more than doubled the town's size, which led to many new houses and streets. Some of the houses were provided for workers by the Humber Cycle Company and some of these still exist on Evelyn Street and Humber Road, at one time called Musco Siko Road. Another interesting housing scheme was a Freehold Land Society, which created a new residential suburb around Devonshire Road.

In 1895 Beeston was one of five areas around Nottingham to be given the status of Urban District, with its own council. Beeston, like other similar areas, already had a Local Board and the new council's powers were much the same at first, but it had options to take on others.

Beeston seems to have been particularly fortunate in attracting new industries and this was again shown in 1902 when the National Telephone Company came to the town. It was later amalgamated with the Swedish firm of L.M. Ericsson and was to be known for many years as Ericssons, one of the town's largest employers. The latter came at an opportune time for employment opportunities as the town suffered a severe blow in 1908 when the Humber Company, then making cars as well as cycles, moved its operations to Coventry. It had employed about 2,000 workers and some of them transferred to Coventry, leaving Beeston with hundreds of empty houses.

Although recovery would have been slow, the

The Beeston Locks were situated near the western end of the Beeston Canal where it joined the River Trent.

extent to which it had recovered can be seen in the 1915 *White's Directory*. Engineering was a major employer with three concerns; the brewery and telephone company were large employers; there were four cycle manufacturers and dealers, probably only small, and a variety of shops and services such as builders and estate agents and there were still four farmers. The textile industry was restricted to only one hosiery manufacturer but lace and lace curtain makers had greatly increased since the turn of the century. The two large tenement factories, Anglo-Scotia and Pollard's, had 17 tenants between them, while there were eight tenants in part of the Humber Works. There were also another five factories and a lace machine builder. Most of the lace factories were to disappear in the next 20 years.

Beeston in 1915 had three banks, two cinemas, 15 public houses and three clubs, including the intriguing Beeston Gravel Pit club. It also had its

own weekly newspaper, the *Beeston and West Notts. Echo* and a motor charabanc ran every hour to Nottingham from 10am to 8pm. The population had doubled in the first decade of the 20th century, with new houses built to accommodate the increase. World War One prevented further development and as elsewhere most younger men joined the armed forces. The shell-filling factory at Chilwell provided work for women.

The 1920s was to be a particularly eventful decade for Beeston. The Urban District Council started to build council houses, but received an unwelcome attempt from the City Council to incorporate the town within its boundaries, together with other similar districts adjoining the city. The proposal was strongly opposed both by Nottinghamshire County Council and the Urban District Council. A public enquiry was held by the Minister of Health and a verbatim report of its proceedings provides interesting reading about life in Beeston. The City Council tried to show up some of the Urban Council's shortcomings. It quoted the district's expenditure on seweraging the streets with water carts as only £546 a year. This gave rise to private enterprise, the junior section, who collected the horse's contribution to gardening and sold it at a penny a pail. What was left, the City Council alleged, was ground to dust by traffic and collected by the lungs of the ratepayers on windy days. The proposal was rejected by the minister, as was a similar attempt in 1932.

More advantageous to Beeston was the transfer of Nottingham University College to Highfields, a large area that adjoined its northern boundary. This provided employment for some Beeston residents and also attracted staff and students to accommodation. The subsequent post-war grant of university status with a great expansion in the number of students and activities has had a similar effect.

The attire of the men on the platform of Beeston Station dates this picture to the Edwardian era, before the level crossing was replaced by a new bridge with its plaque commemorating the official opening. (LSL)

The clear distinction of the boundary between Beeston and Chilwell is on the wall of the Hop Pole public house. Does the boundary divide it?

The Urban District Council's heraldic device at the Town Hall has a bee on it, so the sculpture of the beekeeper and the hive seems quite appropriate on the pedestrianised High Road.

The decision in 1929 by the Boots company to transfer some of its manufacturing activities to Beeston, on a site partly within the city, led to the creation of one of Beeston's most prestigious buildings, designed by Sir Owen Williams. Further architectural innovation in 1966–8 has resulted in another building recognised as of architectural interest as a listed building.

The National Telephone Company employed 130 people on a two-acre site and after Ericsson Telephones took over the number of employees increased to 4,500 in 1939. The site had expanded to 31 acres. The name was later changed to Plesseys and again to GEC Plessey Communications Limited and became part of the multi-national company Siemens.

In 1934 the Urban District's boundaries were extended to include Chilwell, Toton, Bramcote and Stapleford, from a Rural District Council which then ceased to exist. A new town hall was erected in Beeston in 1938 to deal with the enlarged area. Beeston's population in 1931 was 16,017 and the added areas resulted in the combined area having 27,812 people in 6,462 acres. Some idea of the extent of industry in Beeston as extended came in 1937 when a

A quiet corner on West End shows the long garden of one of the houses with the spire of the Methodist Church on Chilwell Road above the trees.

Factories Act required all concerns using machinery to register. The original register had entries for 182 establishments, some of them small such as tailors and hairdressers, as well as the major firms. The register continued for another 30 years and the number registered then was 234.

The post-1945 period has seen changes, especially those necessary to cope with the increase in population. By 1961 it was double the figure of 1931 and this meant new houses, schools, changing patterns of retail shops and leisure facilities. The increase in road traffic has been met by street alterations and pedestrianisation of the main shopping centre. In 1974 Beeston Urban District Council ceased to exist and Broxtowe District Council, which included Beeston, dealt with local government in areas to the north and as far as the Derbyshire border. Beeston, defined as the area of the former Urban District Council, has more than half the population of the borough, as the District Council is now named, with a mayor. Its large industrial and commercial base means that it is an

Only a few hundred yards away from the bustle of Middle Street, this is an almost rural reminder of Beeston as a village.

importer of labour rather than a commuter suburb. It has a diversified appearance with the River Trent and canal on its flatter southern part with hillier and more wooded areas to the north-west.

Its community awareness is widened by a Civic Society and its Local History Society. The bibliography referred to in the introduction has 118 entries, and other publications since then include *Beeston Now and Then* by Judith Church (2001).

BESTWOOD

Bestwood is the most intriguing Nottingham suburb and is the one with the most changes in its history, which goes back for a thousand years, for most of which time it was known as Beskwood. It has no mention in the Domesday Book, yet its name is thought to derive from a variant of an Old English name, *'beosuc'*, meaning 'bent grass', and so the 'wood' where 'bent grass grows'. It is probable that there was no such place before 1066, it being part of the wild country later known as Sherwood Forest which had been part of the royal hunting land. There is also no separate entry for Beskwood in either the Protestation Returns of 1641/2 or the Hearth Tax Returns. This was because it was not a parish, being generally taken to

be part of Lenton parish. The Norman king Henry I gave the monks of Lenton Prior the right to take dead wood and heath from Beskwood, from which it was assumed that it was a detached part of Lenton parish, although the main part of the parish was four miles away.

Dr Thoroton stated that 'It has a very fair lodge in it, and in respect of the pleasant situation of the place and convenience of hunting and pleasure, this Park and Lodge has for many years been the desire and achievement of great men. It is now in lease to William Lord Willoughby of Parham'. He went on to say that it was 'Before the troubles [i.e. the Civil Wars] well stored with red deer'. He also stated that it was in his day parcelled into little closes on one

This picture was taken in 1955 from the junction of Oxclose Lane and Arnold Road, on what a few years later became the Bestwood Park housing estate.

When the Bestwood Park estate was built a sizeable part of the original agricultural land with one of its buildings was developed into Southglade Park.

On the western edge of Bestwood is the River Leen and nearby is the Forge Mill. In 1936 it was occupied by Bayles and Wylie Limited. (LSL)

side, and that much of it had been ploughed, so that there was little wood or venison. Throsby, in his addition, said that in 1790 an old hall was occupied by a Mrs Barton and 'The Park is now thrown in farms'.

The Sherwood Forest survey of 1609 gave details of three properties in what it called Bescott Park. The main holding was the tenancy of the Earl of Rutland of 3,672 acres, while Sir John Byron was the freeholder of 85 acres. He had 11 parcels of land, including an iron mill, mainly let to tenants. After Lord Willoughby died, King Charles II in his death-bed instruction 'Let not poor Nellie starve' gave the park and lodge to Nell Gwynne, the mother of his illegitimate son who was made Duke of St Albans.

White's Directory of 1832 said that the lodge, which had been rebuilt, was unoccupied. It described the land as divided into 13 farms and

stated that some had not been in cultivation until 55 years earlier when a Mr Barton brought a whole colony of his county labourers in and introduced a new system of husbandry. Presumably the Mrs Barton Throsby referred to was Mr Barton's widow.

The 10th Duke of St Albans took a great deal of interest in the Bestwood Park estate and in 1865 a new Bestwood Lodge was completed to the design of S.S. Teulon, an architect noted for his flamboyant style. He also designed Alexandra Lodge Gate and the small Emmanuel Church, all of which survive. After the Duke died in 1898 Bestwood's tenants included Sir Thomas Isaac Birkin, Sir Frank Bowden and his son Sir Harold Bowden. During World War Two the lodge was taken over by the Army, and became a Pay Corps Office. Its stay was extended until 1977 and the lodge was later converted to a hotel.

This photograph of 1881 is of a house party, which included the Duke of Portland as well as the Duke and Duchess of St Albans. (LSL)

In 1869 Bestwood Coal and Iron Company opened a colliery at Bestwood, which became one of the largest employers of labour in the district with over 1,000 employees. Although the company erected its own village, many other miners came from surrounding areas. Hucknall, for instance, was within walking distance. The colliery had two unfortunate accidents in the 1920s. A fire in the headstock to Number 1 shaft fortunately caused no casualties. A more serious and unusual accident in 1929 was the result of a severe frost, which caused water at the side of a shelf to freeze. A sudden thaw caused a large block of ice to fall, killing two men.

In 1930, when 2,000 men were working the colliery, it was worked entirely by electricity, with coal cutters feeding conveyor belts. The colliery still had 94 ponies, which only worked a five-hour day.

The colliery, like most others, was nationalised after the war, but by 1966 it had been working at a loss for four years due to difficult working conditions, and it closed in 1967. Shortly before it closed it

In the 1920s the need to build houses quickly led to new forms of construction being developed. This pair of houses was of a type known as Telford houses at Bestwood village. A similar pair can be seen on Wells Road, Nottingham. (LSL)

At the northern end of Bestwood stands the imposing Bestwood Lodge, built for the Duke of St Albans from 1862 to 1865, in the High Victorian Mansion style. It was designed by architect S.S. Teulon, described in Pevsner's *Nottinghamshire* as 'one of the most ruthless, insensitive and original architects'. It is now a hotel and looks no different from this original architect's drawing.

played a new role as the scene of an ITV series called *The Gamblers*.

In 1878 following the extension of the borough, which included bringing Lenton within the boundary, Bestwood ceased to be part of Lenton parish and was created a parish in its own right. Its southern boundary, which formerly adjoined Basford parish, then adjoined the borough and (from 1897) the city. In the 1920s the City Council started building council houses on a large scale. Most of the new estates were on unbuilt land to the north and north-west of the city. The council started to buy land over the city boundary on which to extend its estates and one of these was on land in Bestwood parish. In 1932 the council was granted another boundary extension which pushed the city boundary in the former Bestwood Park about two miles northwards. The first Bestwood estate was almost completed by 1939, extending along the former Arnold Lane, renamed Arnold Road, from Edwards Lane to Hucknall Road. After the war the council concentrated its house building on the Clifton Estate and in Bilborough. In the mid-1950s it turned its attention to the area to the east of the Bestwood Estate. Although Nottingham already

owned the land, it was unable to start building on the whole site due to colliery workings with the danger of subsidence. It had therefore to phase its operations over a period of years. Arnold Urban District Council also started to build council houses on the eastern boundary until there was no visible distinction between the two authorities. On the pre-1939 estate the City Council built a new grammar school to replace the High Pavement School at Forest Fields. The new grammar school later became a sixth-form college, which has recently closed and moved to a city centre site. The old site is now awaiting redevelopment.

Once Bestwood Park estate, as the post-war scheme was named to distinguish it from the pre-war estate, was completed, the City Council

The tranquillity of Bestwood village came to end when the Bestwood Coal and Iron Company opened its colliery there in the 1880s. The Gothic-style offices could be taken for a church.

A directory of 1899 stated that the colliery employed 1,000 hands 'many of whom necessarily live in the adjoining parishes'. Some of them at least lived in the long street of houses built by the company, with its badge on each.

acquired land to the north, first of all Top Valley and later Rise Park, on which council houses were built. Some private houses were also built. The city boundary then ran parallel with the Bestwood parish boundary, which was from 1974 onwards the Gedling Borough District boundary and has resulted in a similar situation to that at the southern end, on Arnold Road, with city and Gedling estates cheek by jowl. The Bestwood village created by the Bestwood Iron and Coal Company has remained largely unchanged and is surrounded by a rural area. The residents who lived there, in an area which had been known as Bestwood Park for 1,000 years, were not best pleased when the City Council decided to give that name to its new estate.

The loss of Bestwood Colliery and the urban expansion up to Bestwood's boundary resulted in problems such as vandalism and litter depositing in woodland areas. Thanks to energetic action by the appropriate authorities, especially Nottinghamshire County Council, and public co-operation, these have largely between overcome. The creation of a country park, with rangers and public events, and the making of proper footpaths has created an attractive amenity. A notable feature has been the erection of a colliery headstock in memory of the industry which flourished there for nearly a century.

The Local Studies Library in Nottingham has recently compiled a file on Bestwood, which although not published, is available on loan on production of a library ticket. This contains a great deal of information including maps, press cuttings and copies of extracts from various sources on Bestwood.

BRAMCOTE

Bramcote, otherwise spelled as Broncote and Bruncote, means 'cottages in the broom'. The Domesday Book records that William the Usher held the manor, one of only two he had in Nottinghamshire, the other being Trowell. In Bramcote he had one plough and there were four villagers and one small-holder who had three and a half ploughs. The value before 1066 was 60 shillings but in 1086 this had fallen to only 20 shillings. Both the king and William Peverel had jurisdiction in Bramcote over six bovates each.

Dr Thoroton recorded that Herbert de Brampcote, who took his name from the manor, confirmed the rights of the manor as belonging to the monks of Lenton, this grant having been made earlier. Herbert stated that he was 'leaving his heirs the curse of Almighty God and his own, if they should ever attempt to go against his grant.' In the year 1315 he also recorded a similar grant to the nuns of Sampringham. After the dissolution of the monasteries Queen Elizabeth granted the manor to Charles Jackson and his heirs and to William Mason in July 1564. Jackson eventually sold the manor to a man Dr Thoroton names as Richard

The Manor House was known to be in existence as early as 1564, but much of the present building was constructed in the 17th century. It was the home of the lords of the manor until the Sherwins moved to a new house in the early 19th century, and has been occupied by various families since. (LSL)

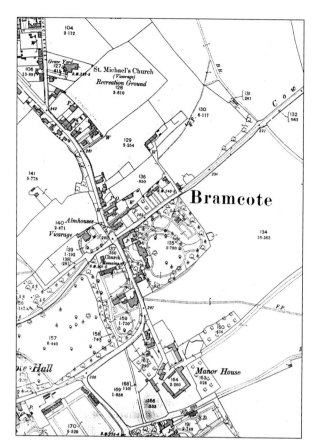

This photograph was taken in the 1930s and is probably at the southern end of Town Street, which retained its village character until fairly recently. (LSL)

Handley, although a more authoritative source said his name was Thomas, not Richard. There was a Yorkshire family named Hanley and it was Thomas Hanley of Wilford who bought the manor. His son Henry is described as 'of Bramcote' and had a son, also Henry, who died in 1650 without an heir, his son Percival having died before him. The burial register of Bramcote invariably spelled the name

Hanley and not Handley, as the members of the family did in inscriptions in their home, Bramcote Manor House.

This picture postcard is inscribed Main Road but there was no such name, as was the case in Arnold. The building on the right looks like a toll house, so it may have been the turnpike road, now the A52. (LSL)

There is a mural tablet to Henry which is in Bramcote church and takes the form of an acrostic:

H eaven holds that soule who tooke such care
E verlasting feasts for others to prepare
N ature ne're taught to doe such excellent things
R eason forbids such acts as damage bringes
Y et these (the fruits of faith) by Hanly done...

The initial letters of the next five lines spell out Hanly.

The tablet records the benefactions that Henry made to several parishes, including one to the town of Nottingham for the erection of 12 almshouses. These were built on Stoney Street and were known as Henry Handley's Almshouses. They were pulled down in 1815 and new ones erected on a site between Wollaton Street and Talbot Street. They were known from then as Hanley Almshouses and the street the same. These were demolished about 50 years ago and the site was valuable enough to allow new almshouses to be built at Bilborough.

When Henry Hanley died the Bramcote estate passed to his brother-in-law Robert Harding, a barrister-at-law, although another Hanley, Gervase of Wilford tried unsuccessfully to obtain it. It was later purchased by a family called Longden. There

This pair of houses at the corner of Chapel Street and Church Street may have been joined to others until they were demolished for road widening.

is an interesting hatchment in Bramcote church, which records the subsequent ownership of the estate. Hatchments show the heraldic symbols of the families who had coats of arms, in this example those of Longden, Gregory and Holden. The hatchment was of John Sherwin Gregory, who died in 1869. He was born John Sherwin Longden and married Catherine Holden. He changed his name to John Sherwin Gregory, the wealthy Nottingham family of that name being related to the Longdens. As he died without children his wife succeeded to the estate, which on her death went to her family, first Captain Henry Holden and then to his son Major E.F. Holden.

The Protestation Return of 1641/2 gives a separate list for Bramcote of 44 names, although it was not a parish. The parish was Attenborough, which also included Chilwell and Toton. Bramcote's list includes Gervase Dodson, vicar, who was also included in the Attenborough list. Bramcote's list included Mr Hanley and Percival Hanley. The Hearth Tax return of 1674 included 21 dwellings, although there may have been others that did not pay the tax. Of the 33 hearths Robert Harding Esq. had seven. That Bramcote was quite small was confirmed in 1796 when John Throsby wrote that it 'consisted of 40 or 50 dwellings and is pleasantly situated.'

By 1831 the population had risen to 562 and was described in *White's Directory* of 1832 as a highly picturesque village occupying several lofty hills and having some large and handsome mansions occupied by their owners. The directory gives the names of seven farmers, eight boot and shoemakers and seven bobbin net makers. It does not, however, mention that a number of men were coal miners. Another name listed is that of William Felkin. He was the grandfather of another William Felkin who became a well-known lace manufacturer in Nottingham where he was mayor for two years, 1850 and 1851. He also wrote the standard book *Machine Wrought History and Lace Manufactures*, published in 1867. His grandfather died at Bramcote in 1836 aged 90 and in his book Felkin describes how he owed much of his later success to his early upbringing, as his own father died young. His grandfather was a frameworker knitter greatly respected at Bramcote.

The 1851 census gives a more complete picture of life at Bramcote. There were 10 lace-makers and 31 framework knitters, several of them being described as glove makers. There were also 45 labourers, most of whom would have been farm labourers. William Henson farmed 217 acres and lived at the Manor House with his wife, five children and six servants. The Sherwin family had

The White Lion public house building dates back to the 18th century. The photograph was taken about 15 years ago and the front garden has since been altered since to make a safer footpath.

sold the Manor House in around 1800 and built a larger mansion, Bramcote Hills, in the north of the village. John Sherwin was then 47 and had eight servants. Another farmer was George Radford with 150 acres. Several families are shown as living at Bramcote Grove, which appears to have been a small exclusive suburb. These included Lawrence Hall, starch manufacturer and magistrate aged 66, John Hadden, hosiery manufacturer and also a magistrate aged 46, and two solicitors John Foxcroft and Richard Enfield. The latter was a member of the Enfield family which provided two town clerks of Nottingham in the 19th century. Richard was one of the men who helped to found Nottingham University College.

Ichabod Charles Wright was the owner of another mansion at Bramcote but he was away from home on the night of the census. His two daughters Fanny, 15, and Sophia, 12, were at home and would have been well looked after by a governess and three servants. Another inhabitant at this time was William Cripps, aged 52, but this was the only census when he lived at Bramcote. He was described as an American merchant, but this did not mean he was of American nationality. It described his trade in cotton from the US, which he frequently visited. He wrote a memoir of some of his Atlantic crossings. He was mayor of Nottingham in 1846. He was born in Newport Pagnell, lived in Nottingham Park for a time, but died in 1884 in

Almost opposite the White Lion is the tower of the 14th-century church, which was left standing when the rest of the church was demolished when a new one was built in 1861.

Devonshire, although his will, made in 1879, was drawn up when he lived in Brooklyn, New York.

Bramcote was obviously an attractive area for wealthier men who worked in Nottingham, as it was near the turnpike road which had been started by an Act of Parliament of 1764, entitled the Bramcote Odd House to Nottingham.

The census also showed that 20 men were employed as coal miners, probably at one of Lord Middleton's collieries at Wollaton or Trowell Moor. Another family had four brothers aged 11 to 20 working as ironstone getters. There were 161 houses in the village with a population of 727.

Bramcote does not seem to have changed very much for the rest of the 19th century, as the recently made available census returns for 1901 show. There were still only 166 houses with a population of 745. Forty-nine miners lived in Bramcote, 18 of them in almost a separate suburb on Chapel Street. A feature of this census was the listing of dwellings of less than five rooms, 88 in all. At the other end of the social scale were the mansions, five of which had 36 servants between them. One of these was Bramcote Hall, the home of Frederick Chatfield Smith, a member of the Nottingham banking family. He had been an MP some years earlier. He was not at home on the night of the census but his wife was, Maud aged 61, and also one son and five daughters, all unmarried, aged between 17 and 35. There were also 17 servants. He had the Hall built in the 1870s on the site of a smaller house and had paid for the building of Chilwell church in 1873. Richard Enfield was still living in Bramcote aged 83 and another well-known personality was Henry John Pearson, the chairman of the Beeston Boiler Company.

The census reveals that 295 of the adult population, that is those over 11 years of age, worked in a variety of trades and professions besides mining. Included in that figure were 104 women, many of them working as lace hands and in other textile occupations, including several shawl makers.

At the junction of Town Street and Cow Lane are four almshouses, erected in 1832 for poor women by Miss Frances Longden.

At this time some women had the vote for local elections, though not parliamentary ones. There were 17 of them in the 1900 register of electors.

Although not a separate parish until this century, being a chapelry to Attenborough, Bramcote had a 14th-century church which was pulled down in 1861 and a new one erected on the opposite side of the road. The tower of the old church still remains. In 1894 Bramcote became part of Stapleford Rural District until 1934 when the Rural District was dissolved. Bramcote then became part of Beeston and Stapleford Urban District, which was incorporated into the Borough of Broxtowe in 1974.

Changes in the village started to take place in the 1930s with some road widening. After World War Two more sweeping changes occurred, mainly on the undeveloped land to the north and west which did not affect the old village too much. Bramcote Hills on the north-west side of the A52 to Derby and Nottingham became a housing estate stretching as far as the boundary with the city. Other new houses on the east side were built towards the Beeston Fields Golf Club. Widening of the A52 and its diversion to by-pass Stapleford resulted in the loss of a few of the older houses and the rebuilding of the Sherwin Arms. Schools and a leisure centre with a swimming pool have been built on land adjoining the former Sherwin mansion, Bramcote

Hills. Bramcote Hall became part of Trent College and later a private school and a more recent new building is the St John's Theological College.

In 1965 the Women's Institute sponsored a competition for institutes to produce a *Scrapbook of 1965*. Bramcote Women's Institute's effort was judged to be the best in Nottinghamshire. It contains much of interest about the history and development of Bramcote, with photographs, press cuttings and details of the various social and cultural activities which reflect the way it has been able to keep its unique character. It can be inspected at Nottinghamshire Archives under reference DD.2645/1.

At the top of a hill on the A52 is Ivy House, with splendid views from the upper windows.

Another view of the countryside, which still exists to the north-west of the former village, can be seen from the recreation ground. The 1965 swimming pool can be seen on the left.

CARLTON

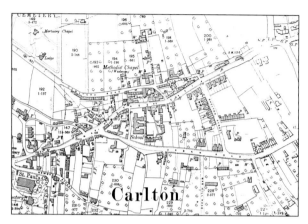

Geoffrey Alselin had a manor listed in the Domesday Book, which was spread over three places, Carlton, Gedling and Colwick, which adjoined each other. Eight hundred years later they were to be combined in one of the newly created urban districts. In between times they had various states of independence. The Domesday Book entry does not therefore provide any separate information about Carlton.

The name, unusually spelled with a K, as Karltun, was from the farm of the carls, common men or husbandmen. The 1609 Sherwood Forest survey provides a good deal of information about the village then. It extended southeastwards from the boundary with the borough on Mapperley Plains, with Gedling to the north. There were 43 separate holdings, one of 43 acres being the town with orchards, gardens, backsides and closes. Six large holdings accounted for 1,122 acres, of which over 1,000 acres were common to Carlton including 149 acres of woodland. The north-western edge of the village was described as Marshall Hill Coppice, from which the present Drive takes its name. It was owned by Sir Henry Pierrepont. The other major owners were Sir John Stanhope, Lord and Lady Stanhope and Sir Francis Willoughby. There were also several small free-holders.

John Throsby in 1790 described the lordship as large and enclosed, owned by the Earl of Chesterfield, the title of the Stanhope family, and Charles Meadows, the owner of Holme Pierrepont who changed his name to Pierrepont. Carlton had no church in 1641 and there is therefore no separate list of its names as they are included with Gedling. The Hearth Tax return for 1664 reveals that Carlton was of modest size with 47 dwellings, 29 of which were not chargeable. There was only one dwelling with four hearths, two with three and all the rest with only one. The 1674 return does not list those not chargeable, but the number of names which were chargeable indicated the number of dwellings, 18. Most of the names in both returns were the same, all the houses but one had two or more hearths, the highest being five, for Mr Henry Freeman.

John Throsby had noted in 1790 that the inhabitants were chiefly engaged in the stocking manufactory. By 1831 the population was 1,704 people compared with the 458 in the village of Gedling. The parish of Gedling consisted of the village and the two townships of Carlton and Stoke

From the slope of the road this picture would appear to be the view taken from the south side of the railway line. Gell's coals is mentioned in early 20th-century directories. There is no mention in any directories of Carlton Cycle and Motor Works, but this was probably entered under the name of the owner, as there were several cycle manufacturers at that time. (LSL)

The Old Volunteer public house on Burton Road is still there but has obviously been rebuilt once. A John Kennedy was the licencee in 1904. (LSL)

Bardoph – both the latter two were without a church. The 1832 *White's Directory* said that the hills of Carlton commanded extensive views of the Trent Valley and that on one of the hills a new village had been built. This was up the hill leading to Nottingham and in the list of inhabitants the names include an asterisk for those living in what is called New Carlton. The list of just over 90 of the main trades included 10 bobbin net makers, four hosiers, eight shoemakers, 19 farmers and five brickmakers. There were large quarries for clay on the hillier part. There had been a Methodist chapel since 1801 and a Baptist one since 1823.

In 1846 the Midland Railway opened a new line from Nottingham to Lincoln with a station at Carlton. While this helped to Carlton by providing

Mrs Ann Maria Godfrey was the occupant of the post office on Main Street in 1899, having succeeded her late husband. By 1910 she was still there but as Mrs Ann Maria Tilley, presumably having remarried. (LSL)

access to Nottingham, it was something of a hindrance, as it still is today, because of a level crossing on the road between Netherfield and Carlton.

The photographer of this view did not provide anything that might give a clue as to the approximate date it was taken. (LSL)

The clothing of the two children on the right and the modern appearance of the shops would indicate a date of around 1910. (LSL)

jurisdiction included Netherfield there were no men living there with a sufficiently valued property to enable them to be members or voters.

The main matters that required the attention of the Board were drainage, sewerage and disposal of refuse, especially from privies and ash pits. As Dr Whitegreave had pointed out, rows of houses had been built without the slightest attempt at sewerage and all the fluid refuse had to be thrown in the streets, which soon became a bog of filth. The Board's work was taken over by an Urban District Council in 1894 and the new body had two wards, Carlton and Netherfield, the electoral system having been extended. In 1883 Carlton was made a separate ecclesiastical parish, with the name Carlton-le-Willows to distinguish it from other parishes in the county with the name Carlton.

The general pattern of economic life in 1900 had not altered very much in the last 100 years. There were still farms and smallholdings, together with small manufacturing concerns mainly in textiles. Quarrying was still being carried on together with brickmaking. The commercial activity was centred round the old village but was tending to spread northwards. The topography of Carlton imposed certain limitations on the shape of development. The main road to Nottingham, a steep hill, sloped away to the north to a valley from which it rose again. On the south side the land again rose steeply from the railway. The area towards the city boundary on Porchester Road was starting to be developed, with a similar development further along Porchester Road, where it met the city boundary on Woodborough Road.

The latter area, named the Porchester Estate, was formed in an unusual manner. The land was formerly Cowdale Farm, the glebe farm of Gedling parish, and in 1886 a group of working men, some

The population continued to increase, especially in the second half of the 19th century. From 1851 to 1881 the population doubled to 4,625 and doubled again by 1901 when it was 10,386. About half the increases were due to the growth of Netherfield, the subject of a separate chapter. By 1864 the bobbin net makers had more or less been replaced by hosiery factories, of which there were 18, mainly small ones.

In 1882 Carlton was sufficiently urbanised to be governed in public health matters by a Local Board. At the first election in February 1882 nine men were elected, all apart from one of whom were from Carlton or Gedling. The other one was Samuel Bourne of Nottingham, whose Britannia Mills gave him the right to be a member. Although the Board's

Nottingham Corporation Tramways provided a service to Carlton just before World War One. The service could not have been very frequent, as it seems to have been a single track at the terminus. (LSL)

of whom had been dispossessed of their allotments, formed a society to create new ones. They were able to purchase 130 acres to the east of Woodborough Road, lying between Porchester Road and Westdale Lane. The allotments were fenced and plots of 600 or 700 square yards were allocated, by ballot, to applicants who could purchase them. Some of them eventually built quite substantial sheds, which they could use at weekends in summer as pleasant retreats. Later when the Urban District Council laid sewers, roads and houses were built on some of the plots. By 1925, 400 such houses had been built, and a residential suburb was created. The names of some of the roads – Haywood, Robinson, Whittingham and Bennett – were names of some of the original committee members of the society.

In the 1930s the suburb spread eastwards as other developments from Carlton resulted in new roads running westwards, such as Valley Road and Cavendish Road, which eventually joined the Porchester Estate. The 1930s also saw the development to the north on both sides of Westdale Lane. In 1938 a new church, St James's, was built on Marshall Hall Drive. This whole development led to a third ward being created on the Urban District Council.

This composite view shows the date to have been around 1910 as the houses on Orlando Drive were built about then. The market seems to have been a small one on the pavement. (LSL)

The trees and hedges around the houses on present day Moore Road indicate the former allotment sites on the Porchester Estate.

More development for housing took place on the south side of Carlton Hill down towards the railway line and this continued after 1945. In 1934 a review of the areas of county districts resulted in an extension of the Urban District Council's area to bring in parts of Gedling and Colwick, increasing the total area to about 4,000 acres. The council was divided into six wards.

Carlton Urban District Council built a number of council houses, as did private builders, with the result that by 1974 it was a mainly residential area. In the 1960s slum clearance of the older part of the area took place with modern replacements of offices, shops, police and fire stations. In 1974 it became part of Gedling Borough Council, which has continued development on similar lines and with the addition of extensive leisure facilities.

The scattered nature of the separate parts of the district, the public transport facilities, the lack of any large industry and the absence of any large open expanses between Carlton, the city and Arnold, have all played a part in it becoming a large residential suburb.

There is little of the rural nature of Carlton remaining and no outstanding architectural features. The authors of the Nottinghamshire volume of the *Buildings of England* series regard the church as the most striking building. This is the parish church of St Paul, built in two stages, 1885 and 1891, a large Romanesque basilica with red and yellow terracotta decoration.

CHILWELL AND TOTON

The origin of Chilwell's name is shown in an alternative spelling of Cidewelle was derived from 'the springs of the cilds' (youngmen). There are

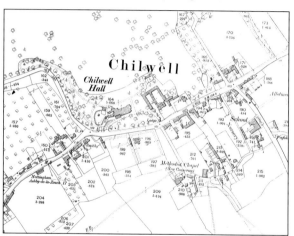

several references to Chilwell in the Domesday Book. Ralph son of Hubert, who had the manor of Barton on the opposite side of the River Trent, also had jurisdiction over Chilwell and East Chilwell where he had one plough and where two freemen, five villagers and 13 small-holders had six ploughs and two ploughing oxen. There were 70 acres of meadow, four acres of underwood, four acres of willow-beds and half a church. This indicates a fairly large manor and a relatively prosperous one, the value with Barton being £5. In East Chilwell, which was land of the King's thanes, owned by special grant, Ernwin had one villager with half a plough and 12 acres meadow. Its value was small, 3s 4d, and was even smaller than before 1066 when

This is one of the older houses from when Chilwell was a small village. Just to the right of the house is an estate of houses built on the site of the former Chilwell Hall. The boundary wall of the grounds still survives.

it was 5s 4d. The separate designation of East Chilwell does not appear subsequently.

Toton, or 'Tofi's farm' had one manor as part of William Peverel's holding where his man, Warner, had three ploughs, four freemen had three bovates of the land and 16 villagers and three smallholders had six ploughs. There was half a church, no doubt shared with adjoining Attenborough, a priest, two mills, 100 acres of meadow and a small willow bed. The value of 60 shillings was unchanged since 1066.

Dr Thoroton mentions two tenants at Chilwell who granted rights there to Lenton Priory. Norman de Mountsautrell gave two parts of his tithes to them, while John Constable of Chester gave them rights to fish from the River Trent. These were described as the first draught of fishes after his steward had his draught. The fish were described as being sperlenes (usually called smelts in Lancashire and Cheshire), which Thoroton thought were gudgeon. John Constable also stipulated that the monks should also have 'whatever in the draught God should bestow in salmon or lampreys'. In a later grant he gave the monks the third draught of fish at Chilwell, together with an acre of land for them to make a dwelling for their servants to look after the fishing. For this privilege they were to have

an anniversary for his father and mother during his lifetime and afterwards for himself. Presumably this would be a special service or prayers. Thoroton gave details of how the manors of Chilwell were held by various families including the Strelleys, Martells, the Earls of Bulgrave, Pymmes and Poutrells. Thomas Charlton purchased the estate at Chilwell from Christopher Pymme and his descendants were to be its owners until the 20th century.

Another of the older houses can still be seen in what was the heart of the village with two public houses.

Both Chilwell and Toton were not parishes, but were townships within the parish of Attenborough. In the 1641/2 Protestation Return they made their protestations at Attenborough Church, but the names were listed separately. Chilwell had 77 names, Toton only 40. Nine names appeared in both places, which is not surprising as they were adjoining each other. Chilwell included Mr Nicholas and Mr Thomas Charlton.

The Hearth Tax returns emphasise the difference in size of the two townships. There were 65 houses at Chilwell in 1654 and 21 at Toton. At Chilwell there were 41 chargeable, with a total of 63 hearths, and 24 not chargeable. Thomas Charlton had 12 hearths, Henry Poutrell four and William New-bricke, his tenant, three. The 1674 return does not give the number not chargeable, but there were 39 chargeable. Thomas Charlton was still the largest payer with 12 hearths.

At the first census in 1801 Chilwell had a population of 638 and Toton 175. *White's*

Directory for 1832 describes Chilwell as a considerable village of 1,450 acres and 892 inhabitants, many of them framework knitters and bobbin net makers. Sanderson's map of 1835 shows the dwellings south of the Hall, on each side of the main road, near the Cadland Inn, which is still there. The occupant of the Hall was Owen Davies MP. The directory recounts how after the Reform Bill rioters had destroyed the silk mill at Beeston they marched to Chilwell threatening to set the Hall on fire. However, Thomas Charlton, the owner, had just died and his body was still in the house. The rioters were persuaded not to attack the Hall. Toton was described as a pleasant village of scattered houses, of 1,200 acres, with a population of 208. Lady Warren of Stapleford was the owner of most of the land. She had provided a schoolhouse and garden, paying the schoolmaster and mistress 12 shillings a week to teach 40 pupils.

By 1881 the population of Chilwell was 1,046 and had expanded towards the boundary with Beeston.

The domestic hosiery industry was being replaced by factories, two of which were Balm Hill and Son, together with E.B. Stephenson and Company, both of whom made Shetland goods. These were mainly shawls, which William Felkin in his book on the history of the lace and hosiery industries described as having been started in 1862 at Hucknall. They were developed on the stocking frame to imitate the similar articles made by hand in the Shetlands. The process used fine woollen yarns in bright colours. Both Hucknall and Chilwell specialised in these, and there was even a special trade union set up known as the Shawl, Fall and Antimacassars Operatives Union. This only folded about 25 years ago, when it had dwindled to a few members, and it had the distinction of being the smallest trade union in the country. Hurt's of Chilwell still make shawls and demonstrate the ancient craft on a stocking frame, alongside modern textile machinery.

By this time another speciality of Chilwell was the horticultural nursery of John Royston Pearson. The population continued to increase modestly up

This more modern house has been demolished to allow for road widening. (LSL)

The building to the left of the Chequers Inn was Neville's tenement factory. At one time the landlord complained to the owners of the factory that vibration from the machinery was causing glasses on his shelves to fall off. The factory was later occupied by Myfords until its demolition a few years ago. O.W. Hemson was the proprietor of the Chequers in the early 1930s. (LSL)

to 1,176 in 1901. In 1897 Chilwell and Toton became part of the newly formed Stapleford Rural District and Chilwell had a parish council. The extension towards Beeston was recorded in a directory for 1899 which referred to several addresses as being in New Chilwell. This included five in Cottage Grove, today known as Grove Avenue.

The number-plate and the style of the coach would seem to date this photograph to the 1960s. (LSL)

Toton continued as a thinly populated area throughout the 19th century. The population showed some rather surprising ups and downs. From 208 in 1831 it fell to 140 in 1851, rising to 193 in 1881 with a sudden increase in 1891 to 245. This was largely accounted for by a block of houses, numbers 1 to 11 Railway Sidings. There were 64 people living in the 11 houses and all the heads of households were railwaymen. Of the whole number of 64 the only ones born in Nottinghamshire were 17 children who had been born at Toton in the previous 10 years. Most of the adults had been born in Derbyshire and Lincolnshire. In the 1871 census William Buxton, a blacksmith, had a wife and three children and nine male lodgers, all unmarried, in their 20s and working on the railway. The marshalling yards had just been established in the 1870s and the railway company later built the 11 houses. They are shown on a 1901 edition Ordnance Survey map right alongside the railway

lines, but are not mentioned in the 1901 census, when the population of Toton was only 186.

The populations of both Chilwell and Toton showed only a small increase by 1911 but the whole life of both was to change in 1915. Robert Mellors, in his history of Attenborough, Chilwell and Toton, published in 1919, describes how in August 1915 Lord Chetwynd, Mr Birkin the land owner and Mr Huskinson his agent might have been seen on the Toton estate near a small wood of oak trees. Their purpose was to set in motion the building of what Mellors describes as a 'gigantic government factory', the Chilwell shell-fitting factory. Lord Chetwynd, the 8th Viscount, was the managing director of the factory from 1915 to 1919. The present day road and barracks are named after him.

The new Chetwynd Barracks, built on the former site of the Ordnance Depot since it closed, has this twin-engine military aircraft on its forecourt.

The factory was completed as a matter of urgency because of the shortage of war ammunition and according to Mellors 10,000 people were employed there. In three years 9,000,000 shells were despatched. To facilitate despatch a branch railway line connected the works with a point on the main line south of Attenborough station. Chilwell will long be remembered for the explosion on 1 July 1918 in which 134 lives were lost. A number of medals of the Order of the British Empire were awarded to rescuers for gallantry, including the rector of Clifton the Revd and Honourable Walter Chetwynd. He was a cousin of

Lord Chetwynd and had been a lieutenant in the Berkshire Yeomanry. He died in 1920.

At the end of World War One the site of the shell-fitting factory became a Royal Army Ordnance Depot, its commanding officer being Lieutenant Colonel Hewell-Jones, after whom one of the roads of today's Chilwell is named.

In 1969 the Chairman of the Beeston and Stapleford Urban District Council presented this charter to the commandant of Chilwell Garrison to mark its appreciation of the cordial relationship between the two organisations on the 50th anniversary of the setting up of the Chilwell Ordnance Depot.

This is known as Long Cottage on the main road through Toton. Formerly two cottages it is probably more than 200 years old.

Chilwell only expanded to a moderate extent between 1918 and 1939, while Toton hardly changed. Both became part of Beeston and Stapleford Urban District from 1935. By 1941, the last *Kelly's Directory* for Nottinghamshire listed Barton's Transport Limited, an iron foundry, a brick manufacturer, a shawl manufacturer, two farmers and two nurserymen. Neville's tenement factory only had three tenants in lace trades, the remaining parts being occupied by two engineering tool manufacturers and a gas meter manufacturer.

There have been extensive railway sidings at Toton for nearly 140 years.

An unusual educational establishment which opened in the 1920s was Boots' College on the High Road, for the further education of their younger employees. Later it became known as Broxtowe College and now it is part of De Montfort University of Leicester, with additional buildings.

Toton still had six farmers and two nurserymen but it also had a textile manufacturer, a motor engineer, the Trent Valley Sports and Social Club and a Kosie Café.

The building in the late 1930s of a by-pass road and widening of the main road to Long Eaton was mainly due to increased road traffic, but was also to be more important to the Ordnance Depot, which greatly expanded during World War Two. The register of electors for Beeston Urban District Council in 1949 was 6,117, including those in Attenborough for Chilwell Ward. This includes 303 living in a section headed Royal Army Ordnance Depot with separate street names, which included NAAFI quarter and Old Married Quarters. The post-war era has seen Chilwell and Toton become residential areas, one merging into the other. This has been accentuated in recent years by the closing down and disappearance of much of the ordnance depot and the building of Chetwynd Barracks. A major physical change has been the taking up of the branch railway line and the disappearance of the road-bridge that crossed the line. A supermarket and a hotel have been built and new leisure facilities provided.

COLWICK

Colwick was one of William Peverel's many manors in the county. He had one plough in lordship, and seven villagers and six small holders had three ploughs. There was also a church and priest, two slaves, one mill, half a fishery, 30 acres of meadow and 15 acres of underwood. It would appear to have been fairly prosperous as its value of 40 shillings was double that before 1066.

Geoffrey Alselin had land in Colwick as well but the entry in the Domesday Book also covers land at Carlton and Gedling. There was also land that the King's thanes held directly from him. Thanes were persons who held land in this way by special grant, usually in return for services. They had two ploughs and one freeman, six villagers and one small-holder with two ploughs, with 31 acres of meadow and eight acres of underwood.

The southern boundary of Colwick was the River Trent and the name from which it was derived was Colici or Colewick, meaning the 'dairy farm of Cola'. The meadows would be ideal for pasture with adequate water. Is it a coincidence that until recently one of Colwick's claims to fame was its Colwick cheese?

The 1609 Sherwood Forest survey map shows that the boundary was Sneinton in the west and Stoke Bardolph on the east. Sir John Byron was the owner of the whole of the parish, his right having been confirmed in 1615 by the commission for defective titles. There were 25 named tenants. Two

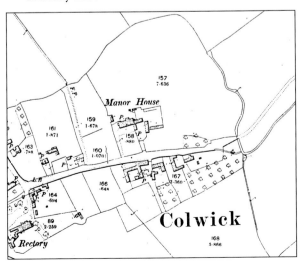

This drawing of Colwick Hall was the work of John Throsby, who in 1790 visited it in connection with his up-dating of Dr Thoroton's 1676 book *The Antiquities of Nottinghamshire*.

of the field names survive to today. Rough Hill Wood adjoined the Sneinton boundary and to the east is Colwick Woods. Candle Meadow gives its name to a housing development at the eastern end of Colwick. The large field, which adjoined Stoke Bardolph, was the Nether (lower) field, which when it was developed in the 19th century became Netherfield.

Dr Thoroton gave details of the ownership from the reign of Henry II when it was transferred from William, who took his surname from the parish, to Sir John Byron, who held it for 500 years. From him Sir James Stonehouse owned it for a short period before the Musters family acquired it. Sir John Musters had been a wealthy London tradesman, one of many from the 17th century who retired to a country seat. In 1776 the Hall was built to the designs of John Carr of York. The kennels so impressed John Throsby that he said it reminded

him in an inverse way of Edwalton – where the priest's dwelling was so dilapidated that it was not even suitable for a dog, whereas here the kennels were fit for a priest to dwell in.

The population in 1641/2 was only small, there

The former parish church of Colwick, dedicated to St John the Baptist, was said to be in a good state of repair in 1936, but five years later it had been abandoned and the roof taken off. In recent years it has been stabilised and made safe.

A new St John's Church has been built in Carlton and the former graveyard has been tidied up. In the background is Colwick Hall.

This picture of Colwick Weir on the River Trent was taken in 1940. It had been made to form a sluice to feed a water mill. After the great flood of 1947 the weir was removed and the river straightened.

being only 14 names on the Protestation Return. One of these was Richard Clarkston, whose family held a farm in Colwick until about 20 years ago. There was little difference shown in the Hearth Tax returns. That of 1664 showed 15 dwellings and for 1674, 16 dwellings. One of the latter must have been quite large with Mr Char. Parrey having 10 hearths. In his reply to Archbishop Herring's enquiry of 1743, Thomas Rose said he did not live in Colwick but at the vicarage house at Colston Bassett. There were then only 10 families and no dissenters.

The population in 1801 was 116 and varied only a little up to 1881 when it was 113. *White's Directory* of 1832 described it as small but

pleasant, with the Hall, half a mile west of the village, being the 'termination of a most agreeable evening's walk from Nottingham'. Besides John Musters at the Hall, there was at least one other house of some size where Charles George Balguy, the Registrar of the Archdeaconry, lived. The list of names consisted of the eight farmers.

The Hall had been the target of the Reform Bill rioters in October 1831, who after setting fire to Nottingham Castle marched out to Colwick and did considerable damage to the Hall. Mrs Musters was said to have been so frightened that she hid in the shrubberies, which it was alleged caused her death shortly afterwards.

The 1851 census, which was the first one to give details of actual ages and more information on

The level crossing on the Midland Railway was built with a crossing keeper's house in 1848. The level crossing is still in use.

occupations and places of birth, showed the population as 120 in 22 dwellings. The Musters had Annesley Hall as their residence and Colwick Hall was let to Isaac Berdmore, a retired (aged 34) builder with four children and two servants. The rector was another member of the Musters family, William. The rectory must have been a large one as he had eight children and 10 servants. The other houses were occupied by farmers, and farm workers. In 1881 there were only two more houses than in 1851, but 10 years later there were 112 with a population of 480. Most of the men were employed on the railway and the additional houses were in Colwick Vale. This was the narrow strip of land between what is now Vale Road and the railway. The older houses, including the Rectory and the Manor, were 100 yards or so to the south, near what is now Mile End Road, and they have all been demolished and the site redeveloped.

In 1881 the Hall was occupied by William Sherbrooke, aged 36, a retired Commander in the Royal Navy with five servants. Ten years later John

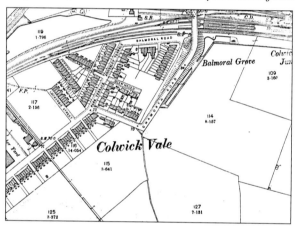

Thomas Forman, aged 43, was living there with three children and four servants. He was the proprietor of the Nottingham newspaper group. The following year the Hall, grounds and the rest of the estate was acquired by Sir Horatio Davies who had already acquired land at West Bridgford and became lord of the manor of both parishes. He immediately sold the Hall and land adjoining to a company, which laid out Colwick Racecourse and turned the Hall into a hotel.

Early in the 20th century, a special station was opened on the Great Northern railway line, for the use of passengers on race days. About the same time, the road from Nottingham was widened and improved and tolls for using it were abolished. The Colwick Vale estate also saw the construction of

two large industrial concerns, William Lawrence and Company, furniture manufacturers, and George Sands, engineers. The population in 1911 was 1,055, rising to 2,305 in 1931.

In 1932 Nottingham City Council was running short of what it regarded as suitable undeveloped sites for building council houses and had already

The Great Northern Railway had a line parallel with the Midland Railway. When Colwick Racecourse was laid out a special racecourse station was built. The railway line was converted to a loop road but the signboard for the station remains between the existing railway and the road.

bought land outside the city boundary adjoining some of its existing estates. This included a part of Colwick Estate on which it was laying out recreation grounds. It therefore promoted a Parliamentary Bill to extend its boundary and was successful in including Colwick, extending about a mile eastwards between Carlton Road and the River Trent. This included the racecourse, Colwick Hall and grounds, Colwick Woods and building land adjoining Carlton Road.

The remaining part of the parish of Colwick, which from 1894 had been part of a rural district council, was absorbed two years later into Carlton Urban District Council. The industrial estate, which had been started north of the River Trent some 20 years earlier, had by 1941 such enterprises as the Anglo-Danish Skin Company, the Anglo-Scottish Sugar Beet Corporation, Armitage Brothers, poultry food manufacturers and three oil companies.

The part of Colwick that is within the city has been changed in several ways in the post-1945

This attractive house was called The Beeches but it has been demolished along with all the other houses in the old Colwick village.

period. Colwick Hall ceased to be used as a hotel several years ago and is now suffering from being unoccupied, vandals having broken in and stolen fireplaces. In contrast, the lake and grounds have been converted into an attractive country park and marina. The area north of Colwick Woods has become a residential area joining to a similar area in Carlton. The former Great Northern LNER railway line from Nottingham to Netherfield has been abandoned and the track converted to a replacement road for the former Colwick Road. This connects with a loop road from the city boundary eastwards for two miles to join the Burton Road, which has facilitated the development on both sides of the road as described in the chapter on Netherfield.

The loop road, the A612, has left Colwick Vale

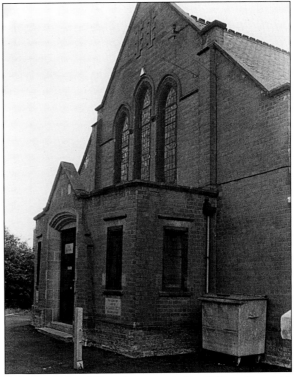

A Congregational Chapel was erected in 1902 on Chaworth Road when Colwick Vale started to grow as a new suburb.

as an island bounded by the railway line. All of the industrial buildings on the north side of Vale Road have been demolished and the sites redeveloped, mainly for housing.

The former parish church of St John the Baptist, which was conveniently close to the Hall, if not for the villagers, has been closed and a new church, St John's, built in a more accessible place. The old building has been made a stabilised roofless structure and the graveyard has been landscaped.

EDWALTON

Edwalton means the farm of Eadweald, an English lord of whom nothing is known. There are two entries in the Domesday Book, where it is described as a manor of Roger de Poitou where there was one plough and one villager and 16 acres of meadow, with a larger manor of Hugh of Grandmesnil adjoining.

He had two ploughs with six freemen and one villager, 15 ploughs and 20 acres of meadow. The value at 20 shillings was double the amount before 1066 whereas the other manor at 10 shillings was worth 30 shillings before 1066.

An owner of land in the reign of Henry II was

Arthur W. Brewill was a Nottingham architect who designed large houses on the land on the west side of Melton Road in the 1890s. This one was Inglewood for Arthur Barnes, a lace manufacturer with a warehouse in Halifax Place, Nottingham. (LSL)

Robert Fitz-Ranulph, whom Dr Thoroton describes as 'one of the foul murderers of Thomas A' Becket'. No doubt in an effort to save his soul, he gave the patronage of Edwalton church to the Abbey of Beauchief. Another owner of land from early mediaeval times was the Chaworth family, which retained the ownership until the 19th century when Mary Chaworth married John Musters, owner of most of the land at neighbouring West Bridgford, who changed his surname to Chaworth-Musters.

Edwalton lay to the south of West Bridgford on more elevated land, which did not have the riverside pastures that Bridgford had. The clay soil would, therefore, not support as large a population as Bridgford. In 1641 the number of adult males signing the Protestation Return was only 29. Included in them were three Hornbuckles and four Pights. In the 1674 Hearth Tax return there were only 16 houses, with only one house with four hearths.

John Throsby, who visited Edwalton in 1790, wrote that a few years before the land was so boggy and indifferent that it could scarcely be let at any price. It had however been much improved by the diligence of the present occupiers. He went on to say that there were 'only 13 farms and as many poor houses'. He regarded the parsonage as one of the most wretched habitations he had ever seen. It

had once been honoured with a thatched covering, but this had been removed by wind and rain.

This echoed similar remarks, in 1743, by the clergyman who wrote in his reply to Archbishop Herring that there was a poor cottage called the parsonage house in which his clerk lived. The clergyman, the Revd John Henson, explained that he was only the curate and did not live at Edwalton, as he was the master of the Free School at Nottingham where he lived.

The gravestone of Rebecca Freeland would not have found favour with the temperance movement.

The parish was quite small, 813 acres, and there had been no need for an Enclosure Act as the land had been enclosed much earlier by agreement. The population in 1801 was 126 and only 130 in 1832 when *White's Directory* gave only a very brief account. It described the church as a humble edifice of brick and quoted the inscription on the gravestone of Rebecca Freeland in the churchyard:

'She drank good ale, good punch and wine,
and lived to the age of 99'

The two ladies standing in front of the 1930s motor car are members of the Burrows family, which had the farm in the background.

She had died in 1761, widow of William Freeland.

As there was no Enclosure Act it was necessary to have a tithe award in 1845 to show what annual payments each occupier should pay, in place of the old system under which, in theory at least, the vicar could expect one-tenth of all the produce of the land. This meant that a detailed map of the village was made and details of its occupants set out in a list, with the amount each had to pay. The map shows that the parish extended on both sides of the turnpike road to Melton Mowbray. The farmhouses and cottages were all on the east side of the road on one street of about a quarter of a mile long, which led past the church to a bridle path to Tollerton.

The total acreage was only 800, and there were eight holdings, which together covered 697 acres. Four of them were of 100 acres or more. Each holding consisted of a number of sites, each numbered and with one number described as homestead, which were the farmhouses and cottages. As the award was drawn up in 1847, it is possible to identify most of the names in the 1851 census

This view of Village Street is dated 1932. The motor car seems to be a different model from the picture of the Burrows family. (LSL)

The Old Post Office was unlikely to have been very busy in view of the small population. It was probably also a farmhouse, which seems to have been extended at the left-hand end.

returns. On four of the farms, there were 13 farm labourers living in their employers' houses, a practice which was starting to die out generally. There were 12 more agricultural labourers living in separate cottages.

The opening in 1869 of a new railway line from Nottingham to London, via Melton Mowbray, was accompanied by a station at Edwalton, the first stop from Nottingham. West Bridgford had declined the honour of having a station. This did not seem to make much difference at first to Edwalton but by 1901 the population had risen to 288. This was due in part to the building of new large detached houses with long gardens set well back from the Melton Road. This development on the west side was from

The Hind Almshouses were erected in 1927 by the family that lived in Edwalton Hall in memory of a son killed in World War One.

Boundary Road as far as the approach to the railway station. Some of the houses had been designed by an architect Arthur S. Brewill, who lived in one himself.

The 1901 census lists 40 residences, 28 of which were on Main Street, most of them the older cottages. There were only two farms and the vicarage. The other houses were the new ones including Inglewood, where Arthur Barnes lived, Edwalton House, occupied by James Bell, a Nottingham bookseller, and the Manor House, where Thomas Shipstone, the brewer who later became Sir Thomas, lived.

Edwalton Station was the first stop on the Midland Railway line, opened in 1879. This was another line for the company, which had opened the first Nottingham to Derby line in 1839. The line through Edwalton went to Melton Mowbray and London. (LSL)

The 1920s and 1930s saw a modest expansion of the former village into a residential suburb. Mainly detached houses were built along Melton Road past the railway station and on the east side of the road from Valley Road to Village Road. Croft Road, Wellin Lane and Hallfields were laid out but only as cul-de-sacs at that time. Members of the Hind family, descendants of the first clerk to the Nottinghamshire County Council, Jesse Hind, lived at Edwalton Hall and erected the Hind Memorial Homes in memory of a member of the family killed in World War One. In 1934 the Urban District of West Bridgford was expanded by taking in Edwalton. The outbreak of war in 1939 meant that this resulted in little change in Edwalton.

After the war, Edwalton started to expand with new roads, houses, schools and shops including a large number of council houses. The former residence Edwalton Hall became a hotel, which is now being converted into housing. A new church, St Luke's, was built and later a separate ecclesiastical parish was formed. The expansion gradually led to the disappearance of the separation between Edwalton and West Bridgford, although the former still retains its own identity. The creation of a new by-pass road, part of the A52, on the eastern edge has led to the building of new housing at Gamston with new roads joining Edwalton.

The railway line was closed in 1969 and a new school built on the western side of the track followed, after the Urban District Council was absorbed into Rushcliffe Borough, by a leisure centre and swimming pool. A municipal golf course has been laid out to the east of the parish church.

The Old Rectory stood where Paddock Close has been since it was demolished. (LSL)

GEDLING

The first part of the name is a personal one, Gedel or Geala, so it was the home of people of his tribe. In the Domesday Book, Roger of Bully, like William Peverel a holder of many manors in Nottinghamshire, had a manor in Gedling with two ploughs, while nine villagers and two small-holders had two ploughs. There was 10 acres of meadow, with woodland pasture two furlongs long and one furlong wide. The value had increased from 32 shillings before 1066 to 40 shillings.

Geoffrey Alselin also had a manor and jurisdiction over another area, in both cases Gedling sharing with adjoining parishes. The manor, which included Stoke Bardolph as well, was a large one. In addition to Geoffrey, who had one plough, there were 15 villagers, six slaves and 21 small-holders. There was also a priest and a church, a fishery, two mills, 30 acres of meadow and woodland pasture three furlongs long and one wide. The value before 1066 was £5 10s 0d and had increased to £6. Alselin's other holding was spread over Gedling, Carlton and Colwick, which were to be united 900 years later. Thirty freemen had 10½ ploughs with meadow and underwood.

Gedling was in Sherwood Forest and the 1609 survey and map gave details of 35 holdings. The eight largest of these totalled 3,231 acres, of which Sir John Stanhope had four woodlands of 294 acres. The remainder was all common to Gedling and in some cases to Stoke Bardolph as well. The 'towne' covered 85 acres, with orchards, gardens, and backside closes. The landowners were the Earl of Shrewsbury and Sir John Stanhope.

The Protestation Return of 1641/2 gives 204 names, which included Carlton, as this was not a parish then. Of the 204 adult men, there were only

The caption on the postcard merely says Gedling, Notts, but the appearance of the shops would point to Main Road. The fashion show of juvenile clothing was no doubt of Edwardian vintage. (LSL)

The Memorial Hall is at the junction of Main Road and Arnold Lane. It is the church hall and was erected in 1924, paid for by Lieutenant Colonel Blackburn and his wife who lived at Gedling Manor.

119 different surnames, which probably indicated that there was not much movement outside the parish. Gedling was quite a lot bigger than most local areas.

The Hearth Tax return of 1664 showed that there were 71 dwellings, all of which except one had just one hearth. The exception was Lawrence Palmer, minister, who had six hearths. Ten years later in the 1674 return there were 73 dwellings but a surprising feature is the number which had two or more hearths – 30. Mr Palmer still had six, as had Mr Trewman, who was not in the 1664 return. Twenty-four of the names in the 1674 return do not appear in the list of 1664.

Dr Thoroton does not give a complete account of

There is little to indicate when this photograph was taken but it has a modern look, say 1950s, compared with Edwardian postcards. From the position of Gedling's famous spire, the viewpoint would be near Hardy's Drive and Main Road. (LSL)

the ownership of the lands but gives details of a grant by the King in 1539 to Michael Stanhope and his wife Anne of many lands and manors, including Gedling, which had been formerly owned by Shelford monastery. The Stanhope family, later ennobled as Earls of Chesterfield, became owners of large estates in Nottinghamshire. John Throsby in his additions to Thoroton mentioned two old stone coffins, which he said lay near the surface of the earth, in which persons other than the original occupiers had been laid.

He was told that one gentleman who was too tall to fit the coffin was thrust in to make him fit it. He also referred to a stone in the churchyard, which had the inscription 'Here lieth the body of Joseph

The highly decorated drinking fountain was presented to the village in 1874 by the Countess of Carnarvon, the wife of the 4th Earl of Carnarvon who owned land at Gedling and elsewhere. The Countess, who died the following year, was formerly Lady Evelyn Stanhope, daughter of the Earl of Chesterfield.

The steeple of All Hallows church has been described as one of the most remarkable in the county – historically, visually and archaeologically. The slim spire takes up more than half the steeple.

Smalley, whose mother was 60 years old when he was born'.

Gedling's parish church was also the church for two townships, Carlton and Stoke Bardolph. At the first National Census of 1801 Gedling's population of 554 had already been outstripped by Carlton with 819. *White's Directory* of 1832 lists three bobbin net makers where as Carlton had 10, as well as four hosiers and five brickmakers. Gedling House, an elegant 18th-century mansion, was owned by William Elliott Elliott, who had inherited a fortune earned by his father from a secret formula for dyeing lace. A large workhouse had been built

in 1787 to accommodate the poor of 30 parishes. *Morris's Directory* of 1877 could add little to the history of the previous 45 years, apart from 'a handsome fountain in the centre of the village, with seats on either side, was presented by the late Countess of Carnarvon in 1875'.

An event out of keeping with Gedling's rural character was the sinking of Gedling Colliery in 1902, which was a mile away from the old village and did not spoil its appearance. At the census of 1901 the population was still only 759. By 1921 it had increased to 1,869, with new houses built along Westdale Lane up to Mapperley Plains. There was still little industry apart from the colliery and most

This dramatic view of Gedling Colliery was taken in around 1950 and emphasises the sharp contrast with the surrounding countryside. (LSL)

An attractive pair of older houses at the Arnold Lane end of Main Road.

The spoil heap is the only reminder of the 1902 colliery, which closed a few years ago.

of the land in the northern part was open country, with a golf club on Mapperley Plains. The Kennels

of the South Nottinghamshire Fox Hounds were also in Gedling.

In 1935 Gedling became part of Carlton Urban District Council and its history since then is more or less of extension as a residential suburb largely indistinguishable from Carlton. The disappearance of Carlton Urban District Council in 1974 and its absorption by Gedling Borough Council no doubt caused quiet satisfaction to those who were aware of the earlier days when Carlton was only a small part of Gedling.

There is still farmland and open space at Gedling. The colliery has gone, and there is, as yet, no firm proposal for what will happen to its site.

HUCKNALL

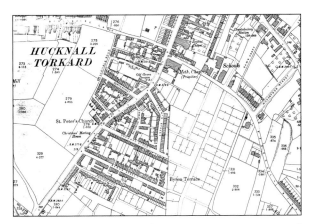

The name is derived from 'Hucca', a personal name and '*healh*', an angle of land. In the Domesday Book the Normans wrote it as 'Hochenlale'. There were two manors, one held by William Peverel and the other by Ralph of Buron (the name later becoming Byron). Neither of them appear to have been very prosperous in 1086, both having values only half of what they were before 1066. William Peverel's manor only had three villagers with one plough, while Ralph's manor had one plough and five villagers had three and a

half ploughs with woodland pasture one league long and half a league wide.

Hucknall became known as Hucknall Torkard as early as the 12th century, to distinguish it from a nearby village of the same name. The name came from Geoffrey Torcard, who is first recorded in 1195. He left a bequest to Lenton Priory giving the monks the right to have one cart continually wandering about to gather up the dead wood of Hucknall.

There is no reference to Hucknall in the 1609 Sherwood Forest survey, although it adjoins several places which were. The Protestation Return of 1641/2 lists 112 adult men with 66 separate names. The 1664 Hearth Tax return has not survived but the one for 1674 has, and lists the names of 61 occupants paying tax, though there may have been occupiers of other dwellings who did not pay the tax. Most of the dwellings had only one or two hearths, but a Mr Flower had eight and William Byron Esq. had 14. This was Bulwell Wood Hall.

161

This picture was taken before 1897. Although the caption states 'Church' there is only a shadowy glimpse of it. What it does show is a very interesting view of what life was like on High Street. (LSL)

Hucknall No.1 colliery as photographed in around 1897. (LSL)

Dr Thoroton gave details of ownership and tenancies since Norman times, which he said had passed through many hands. He reckoned that at the time he was writing there were four or five manors and he gave the owners names such as the Honourable William Byron, the Earl of Essex, Lancelot Rolleston and a man named Curtis. He added that the principal part of the township was in the inheritance of Lord Byron. When John Throsby visited Hucknall in 1790 to compile his additions to Thoroton's work, he attributed the principal ownerships to the Duke of Portland, Lancelot Rolleston, John Newton and others. He also noted that there were 200 dwellings in a long street.

The population in 1801 was 1,497 and by 1832, when *White's Directory* was published, it was 2,200. The directory described it as a large but indifferently built village, principally, as Throsby had indicated, of one long street. Many of the inhabitants were frame work knitters occupying small

This windmill was called Club Mill. This probably refers to a form of partnership between various farmers who could use it to grind their corn. (LSL)

farms. This was a typical community, which had grown in the 18th century with the spread of the domestic knitting frame, which could be worked at times when work was not possible on the land. The directory listed 40 farms and 13 hosiery agents.

Thirty years later *White's Directory* described the village as considerable and well built. In 1861 it had 661 houses and 2,836 inhabitants. The economy had changed little in the intervening years, and in 1864 there were 37 farmers and 36 hosiery agents and manufacturers. The latter were now principally engaged in making woollen and silk shawls. This was a recent development, which William Felkin, the 19th-century historian of the lace and hosiery industries, described as having

been introduced in 1862 by an intelligent workman at Hucknall, W. Farrands. He made shawls in imitation of hand-knitted Shetland shawls on the stocking frame.

The 1864 directory included in the list of names of the principal inhabitants Walker and Ellis, colliery owner. This was the Hucknall Colliery Company, the partners being Edward Shipley Ellis, his brother Alfred, his son John Edward Ellis, and William Walker. The sinking of a coal shaft had begun in 1861 and by 1862 No.1 and No.2 collieries were being worked. This was an important event, which was to affect Hucknall's history for over 100 years. It was also important for another reason. John Edward Ellis, the 20-year-old

The licencee of the Chequers public house on High Street was Josiah Ball from about 1901 to 1909. There is a still a Chequers on High Street. The style of clothing shows a wide variety. (LSL)

son of Edward senior, who was then chairman of the Midland Railway, soon became manager of the colliery and was to become a dominant figure in Hucknall, and beyond, for the next 50 years.

Despite the importance of this change in Hucknall it was not without its problems, both then and later. An early dispute between men and management led to a lock-out in 1866 and a fire in one colliery led to it being flooded.

By 1881 the population had reached 10,023 and a third colliery had been opened in nearby Linby. There would not have been sufficient men to work the collieries in Hucknall itself and others came from adjoining areas. This was assisted by the opening of the Midland Railway with a line through Hucknall in 1848. Later the Great Northern Railway built a line, as did the Great Central by 1901. Hucknall then had four stations.

The period from 1867 to 1881, as well as the growth in population, saw improvement in the way of life generally and John Edward Ellis played a large part in this. A Local Board of Health was started in 1867, Ellis becoming chairman, an office he later held on a School Board as well. In 1876 the Local Board levied rates of £1,305 to pay for highways, lighting, paving and drainage, a considerable sum in relation to the number of ratepayers. In this period a co-operative society was formed, which besides retailing ran a clothing factory and purchased land for the building of houses. A savings bank was also started. The nonconformist chapels and the church increased their influence, with a temperance movement and cultural activities, especially musical ones.

In 1885 Ellis was elected as MP for the Rushcliffe Division, which included Hucknall, a position he held until just before his death in 1910. Working men were given the right to vote without a property qualification and were able to vote for members of the County Council in 1888 and for the Urban District Council in 1894, Hucknall being one of the original councils under an Act of that date.

This was Bulwell Wood Hall in 1929, which was destroyed by fire in 1937. It was for many years a seat of the Byron family but in 1937 it was let to a tenant farmer. (LSL)

By 1901, when the population was 15,250, the collieries were the largest workplaces, while hosiery provided work in six factories and shawl manufacturers numbered eight. There was also a cigar factory, which provided work for 400 people. All these trades were soon affected by times of economic depression and, in the case of collieries, by disputes. The town did not have any lace factories, which at this period were large employers in Nottingham and adjoining districts. The lace trade was still relatively prosperous and wages were good, especially for skilled workers. The increased railway provision no doubt encouraged women from Hucknall to travel to work daily.

Living conditions in Hucknall were far from ideal with obsolete waste disposal by privy middens and ash pits, high infant mortality and deaths from infectious diseases linked to poor housing conditions. These things were of course common to all industrial towns, Nottingham itself being just as bad in some parts.

Whether the employment opportunities and living conditions were a factor or not, the population in the first 10 years of the 20th century increased only marginally from 15,250 to 15,870. In the same period the four urban districts of Arnold, Beeston, Carlton and West Bridgford had a total increase of 43% from 34,776 to 49,695. Even

Nottingham increased its population by 20,000, although this was only 8.4%.

From 1919 to 1939 the population increased by just under 20%, from 16,834 to 19,890, most of which took place in the 1930s. The Urban District Council started to build council houses and to demolish some of the worst older houses. Private houses were also built, including some for owner-occupation. A clinic was opened in 1930 for health visitors and infant welfare provision and a mains sewerage plant was started. Some new industries were established and Rolls-Royce moved to the aerodrome, which had been opened during World War One. Two amenities were provided with assistance from the Duke of Portland and Sir Julian Cahn, a public park and a group of almshouses.

These houses were scheduled for demolition in 1934. They were on North Hill off Annesley Road. (LSL)

After World War Two, Hucknall made considerable efforts to improve housing conditions by further slum clearance and increased numbers of both council and private houses. In 1891 the population of 13,094 lived in 2,513 houses, an average of just over five people per house. By 1971 the population was just double that of 1891, but the number of houses was nearly four times as many, at 9,064, with an average occupancy of less than three. This had been achieved by building new estates, which have increased the built-up part of the town.

In 1974 the Urban District Council, like all the others, ceased to exist and the town became part of

Broomhill Cottages are on the west side of Nottingham Road in what was a hamlet of that name, just under a mile from the city boundary.

St Mary's churchyard is a quiet oasis only 100 yards from the bustle of Hucknall's shopping streets.

Ashfield District Council. The last quarter of the 20th century has seen major changes in Hucknall's appearance and economic life. The closure of the railways and the four stations, along with the closure of all the collieries, was followed by redevelopment of those sites. This has altered the landscape, as has the opening of a by-pass road to cut down traffic through the town's 'long street' described by earlier writers. This remains largely unchanged, without the extensive pedestrianisation of other areas. The hosiery, shawl and cigar factories have all gone, and even some of the 1930s industrial buildings have disappeared.

New leisure centres, a sixth-form college and new light industries have been built but the town's work structure has changed radically. The reopening for passenger traffic of one railway line and station, the Robin Hood line, with a large car park, and a frequent bus service, have contributed to Hucknall becoming more of a residential and services suburb. The end of 2003 is scheduled to see the opening of yet another stage of Hucknall's history, the Express Transit, a modern tramway.

NETHERFIELD

One of the field names of Colwick parish shown on the 1609 Sherwood Forest survey map was the Nether Field, or lower field. It was on the east side of the parish bordering Stoke Bardolph. Until the middle of the 19th century there were no buildings there and no people living there. The building of the Midland Railway through Colwick with a station opened in 1848 resulted in a few buildings being erected in the Nether Field and in the 1851 census there were 68 people living there. By 1881 there were 735 people. The reason for this tenfold increase was the coming of the railways.

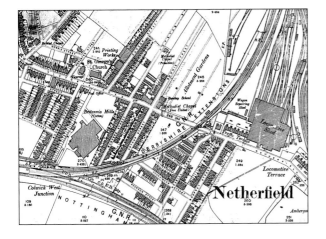

The toll-gate on Meadow Road was erected by the owners of Colwick estate but was removed at the beginning of the 20th century.

Shortly after the Midland Railway opened its line to Lincoln another smaller company started to build a line intended to link Ambergate in Derbyshire, through Nottingham and Grantham, to the east coast. In the event only a 22-mile stretch from Grantham over the River Trent via Radcliffe to a point adjoining the Midland Railway was built. The company had an arrangement with the Midland Railway to use its lines to Nottingham. In the 1850s the company was taken over by one of the Midland Railway's main rivals, the Great Northern. The arrangement with the Midland Railway to share its line to Nottingham then proved to be unsatisfactory, so the Great Northern built a new line. This started at a new Nottingham Station, the low level on London Road. The line then ran parallel to the Midland Railway until it joined the existing line to Grantham. This section, although it was in Colwick parish, was close to the Nether Field. A feature of this field was a carriageway from

This more recent photograph of Meadow Road shows how it developed after the toll-gate was removed.

The LNER railway at Netherfield station had two tracks. The one on the right went to Grantham, the other one northwards as part of the Derbyshire extension. (LSL)

the River Trent northwards to Gedling, was laid down in accordance with the award under the Gedling Inclosure Act of 1795. Colwick, Carlton and Gedling were all included in the Inclosure Act. The new road followed what had been a trackway for centuries.

Houses for the railway workers were built on this carriageway, which became the spine road of a new village with other streets running off on either side. A major development from 1871 onwards was the decision of the Great Northern company to expand its activities to try to obtain the coal trade with the Erewash Valley collieries on the border of Nottinghamshire and Derbyshire. To do so it built another new line, the Derbyshire and Staffordshire extension. This started with two short stretches of line from the existing line, about two thirds of a mile apart, northwards, which then amalgamated. The line then turned north through Gedling and on to Daybrook and westwards from there.

The growing demand for coal meant increased work for the Great Northern and in 1875 it started to build a marshalling yard to the south of the new Derbyshire extension lines. This was to become the largest yard of the GNR in the region, its construction taking place over the next 25 years. It became a hive of activity for the repair and maintenance of engines and wagons. It was joined in this enterprise by the London and North Western

The building with the tower on 3 Chandos Street was erected in around 1910.

Railway, which was able to use the new line to the north for iron ore from the Leicestershire area and return with coal over its own lines to Peterborough and London.

This increased industrial activity was responsible for an increase in population, reaching 4,646 by 1901 and a peak of 7,104 in 1921. The area became known at Colwick Loco until 1883 when the Carlton Local Board ruled that the part of Carlton south of the Midland Railway should be known as Netherfield. The railway development was no doubt a factor in other industries opening new premises in the town. The largest of these was the Britannia Mills, erected for the cotton-doubling firm of Samuel Bourne and Company. Samuel Bourne had started a similar firm in Nottingham in 1869 to meet the demand of the growing lace and hosiery trades for double-strength yarn instead of single, which the Lancashire firms could not provide with prompt service. His decision to move to Netherfield was on economic grounds as land there would be cheaper with more available for expansion. The existence of two railway stations would help attract workers, mainly female, as there would be few available in the town at that date.

Another large employer and one of an unusual character was Stafford and Company, a printing firm. It moved its premises, which had been in Nottingham since 1845, to Curzon Street in Netherfield. The firm specialised in theatrical and other posters, many of them designed by their own lithographic artists. By 1892 they had a workforce of 130 people.

The census enumerator's returns from 1871 to 1901 reveal the unique aspect of the closed community of what was essentially a railway town. In the earlier years they reveal that most of the adult men were railway workers who had been born in other counties with wives similarly from outside and many with young children. One effect of this was that most railway men's wives did not work and there were not enough girls to be employed in Bourne's mill, so his workforce was one which travelled daily, mainly from Nottingham. The later censuses also show how sons as they grew up tended to follow their fathers to work on the railway.

The way in which the community was self-sufficient in some ways was illustrated by the fact that by 1902, despite the sizeable population, there was only one public house in Netherfield, the Railway Hotel. There was also a Netherfield Railway Club, which would no doubt account for this. The adjoining district of Carlton had nine public houses.

The street names reveal the character of Netherfield's development. There was a Traffic Terrace, Locomotive Terrace and North Western Terrace. Bourne Street was next to Britannia Mills, and Manvers Street and Carnavon Street reflected

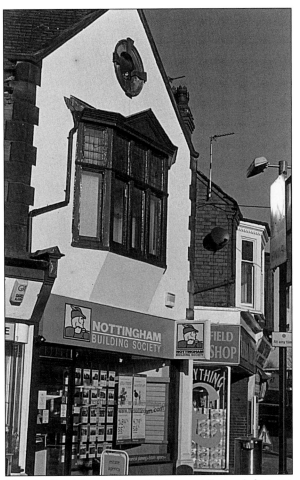

Victoria Road has rather pleasing architectural features compared to most of the other buildings.

the aristocratic landowners. Curzon Street was not named after the Kedleston family, but after a Nottingham man and his sister who owned property in the town.

The increasingly urban nature of Netherfield by 1902 is shown by some of the professions and trades there. There were three house and estate agents, a bank, two cabinet-makers, two chemists, two dentists, two music teachers, a pawnbroker and a photographer. A number of these were not available at Carlton so Netherfield must have been quite a busy centre.

Netherfield continued to be a growing industrial suburb for the first two decades of the 20th century, although its progress was marred on two occasions by strikes. The first, of railway workers, did not affect the town too much, but a coal miners' strike a year later caused a more serious setback when the railways were not moving coal. This period saw a welcome improvement when a toll gate was removed from the road through Colwick and Nottingham.

The 1920s saw an end to the continued expansion of the town, as both the growth of electricity for power and the use of motor vehicles reduced the demand for coal and railways. Although Bourne's managed to expand its business some of this was met by acquiring more premises in Lancashire. World War Two saw the mills at Netherfield requisitioned for war production.

The second half of the 20th century was marked by the gradual but complete demise of the three major industrial enterprises. The railways were nationalised in 1947 and subsequent reorganisation of the industry resulted in the closure of the marshalling yard. This enabled the Colwick loop road to be built with a retail park on the far side of the road. While this has removed through traffic from the older parts of Netherfield and Colwick it was of little immediate benefit to them.

Bourne's mill managed to cope with changing conditions in the textile industry, but like much of the industry it could not compete with cheaper labour in other countries. After amalgamation with other firms, Britannia Mills was demolished in

Kozi Kots. The unorthodox spelling of this small group of houses off Victoria Road was no doubt intended to give it a modern image. Ideal for trainspotters, the railway runs just behind the fence.

1982 and the site used for the erection of a sheltered housing complex.

The printing firm of Staffords continued until 1961 when it was taken over. It succeeded for nearly 30 years until over-production in the printing industry caused it to close. The old building was demolished and the site used for a Housing Association scheme.

The rise and fall of industrial Netherfield thus took a little over 100 years. There has been some new housing and new small industrial and service building, but Netherfield remains a mainly residential suburb with much Victorian and Edwardian housing.

STAPLEFORD

Stapleford must be one of the few places whose name is spelled in the Domesday Book as it is today. It means a ford (presumably over the River Erewash) marked by a post or staple. Part of William Peverel's empire, the one manor at Stapleford was held by Robert from him with three ploughs. There were six villagers with six ploughs, two slaves, a priest and a church and 58 acres of

meadow. The value had fallen from 60 shillings before 1066 to 40 shillings.

Dr Thoroton devotes six pages in his book to Stapleford and has a genealogical table of the lords of the manor through 20 generations starting from the Normans down to his own time. He assumes that the Robert mentioned in the Domesday Book was a de Heriz. Later descendants assumed the

The Wesley Chapel on Nottingham Road was one of Stapleford's early nonconformist chapels. John Wesley visited Stapleford in 1774 and mentioned in his diary that he preached there in a field near Bob's Rock.

name de Stapleford until in the 14th century Sampson died without issue and the lands went to John Teverey, who married Sampson's sister Margareta. The Tevereys lasted for seven generations until the manor again passed through marriage to Sir Byron Palmes. A descendant, William, who inherited the manor, married a daughter of Lord Evers and so obtained her estate as well. Dr Thoroton said that William Palmes liked Yorkshire and sold his old house at Stapleford to Arthur Warren, son of Arthur Warren of Toton.

It appears that the lands had been sold to various other owners, one of whom, a widow of Robert Matley, had inherited the third part of a water mill. Dr Thoroton supposed that this part belonged to his cousin Hollingworth, who had the water mill and considerable lands in the town. This relationship perhaps explains Dr Thoroton's considerable knowledge of Stapleford's ownerships. He also gave the names of seven owners of land in 1612.

The Protestation Return of 1641/42 listed 67 names with 46 different surnames, indicating that the popu-

lation would have been about 250. The Hearth Tax Return for 1674 lists 34 names with one house having nine hearths. This is described as belonging to William Palines Esq., but this is probably a transcription error for Palmer, spelled Palmes by Dr Thoroton. In 1743 the number of families were estimated at 50 in the return to Archbishop Herring. In 1771 an Enclosure Act was obtained, of 986 acres which also included Bramcote, although a number of property owners opposed the proposal saying it would be of no use to them.

Stapleford was on the road from Nottingham, which was turnpiked in 1780 and was near to the Erewash Canal just across the border with Derbyshire. This would have helped communications, and would have proved useful when the village, like most others in the area, became part of the framework knitting industry. By 1801 the census figure of population was 748, nearly as much as Beeston, which had the advantage of being nearer to Nottingham.

The population had more than doubled by 1831 and *White's Directory* a year later stated that there were upwards of 100 machines employed in making tatting and warp lace. It also recorded that some of the inhabitants lived at New Stapleford a mile

Not far from the former Wesley Chapel on the opposite side of Nottingham Road is this group of houses with the upper windows designed to give plenty of light for working on stocking frames.

Known as the Stapleford Sphinx, this is one of four such figures, which formed the feet of a sarcophagus. Two of them can now be seen at the side of St Helen's church door. The sarcophagus was erected in memory of Captain William Sleigh, an army officer who died in 1842. (LSL)

As the inscription over the arch tells us, Stapleford Cemetery was the gift of Joseph Fairfield, a lace manufacturer who lived in the town where he had a factory.

north-east of the village, near the Hemlock Stone, 'a ponderous fragment of a Druid's Temple'. The latter was only one explanation of the origin of this landmark, another being that the Devil had been upset by the Prior of Lenton and had thrown this large rock at him, but it fell short of its target.

The directory named the principal owners as Lady Warren, Mrs Fisher, Mr Charles Antiel, Mr John Dodsley and John Jackson Esq., the lord of the manor. Lady Warren was the widow of Admiral Sir John Borlace Warren who died in 1825 and who had a distinguished naval career. The directory recounts how at the start of the American war he visited the London prisons and paid the outstanding debts of any naval officers who had been imprisoned. He rebuilt Stapleford Hall in 1797.

The population increased only slowly between 1831 and 1871, but the rate of increase accelerated from then on. A branch of the Erewash Valley railway line had been established earlier and this was to enable Stanton Iron works to expand. Although over the border in Derbyshire, it was near enough to attract workers from Stapleford, as was the Trowell Moor colliery. More important was the transition in the lace industry from the stocking frame to factories. Manufacturers in Nottingham were complaining that high wages in the trade there

were forcing them to build new factories in such places as Long Eaton and Stapleford where wages were lower. Prominent in this respect at Stapleford was Joseph Fearfield, who built a large factory that survived for many years. The 1870s saw an increase of 60% in population, together with the establishment of a co-operative society, a School Board and a Burial Board, with a cemetery paid for by Joseph Fearfield. The Albert Hall was built as a meeting place, and users included a Literacy Institute. A Baptist chapel was erected in 1875, alongside the existing four Methodist chapels.

In 1895 Stapleford became the headquarters of a Rural District Council covering Bramcote, Chilwell and Toton and had a parish council. By 1903 the population of Stapleford was estimated at 7,560, an increase of 2,000 over 1901. By the time war broke out in 1914, although the population had not increased very much, there were a number of developments which had taken place in the period

This sketch by Nigel Brook is of what was the Chambers Pencil factory from 1913 to 1973, but which was demolished. Before that it had been Joseph Fairfield's factory.

since 1901. Fearfield's lace factory had closed and the building was used by F. Chambers and Company, a lead pencil manufacturer. A Carnegie Free Library, a picture palace, a recreation ground, a police station and a Fire Brigade were all in existence. There were two banks, a freehold land society and the Derbyshire and Nottinghamshire Electric Power Company had premises on Nottingham Road. The proximity of Sandiacre, just across the Erewash in Derbyshire, enabled the two communities to join together in a joint sewage works and water company.

There was little change in population in the post-1918 period, the figure for 1931 being only 300 more than in 1911. The lace industry had been in decline since 1914 but some hosiery concerns opened in Stapleford. There were few major changes too, in the 20-year inter-war period, such alterations as there were being in line with other areas. There were two cinemas, motor garages, the Carr Fastener Company, a motor car body fitters and a wireless shop.

In 1934, a review of county district areas made changes arising from the altered patterns since 1894 of some areas. The Stapleford Rural District was dissolved and its four constituents absorbed into a newly named Beeston and Stapleford Urban District. This made little difference to Stapleford for

some time, especially up to 1945. From then on, changes were to be in line with the enlarged area, although these did not affect Stapleford perhaps as much as Chilwell with Beeston. The topographical layout was such that assimilation of Stapleford was not as easily noticeable as in the rest of the district. The A52 by-pass road and open country to the east meant a physical separation from the rest of the former urban district council.

Since the 1950s there has been a considerable increase in new house building, stretching northwards as far as the Ilkeston Road and southwards as far as the A52. Since 1974 Stapleford has become part of Broxtowe Borough Council and has its own Town Council, the successor to the parish council. The latter part of the 20th century has seen the demolition of some of its notable buildings, Stapleford Hall, Manor House and the former Fearfields/Chambers factory as well as some of the older houses. Other buildings have survived with new uses. The Carnegie Library is now a civic and community centre and the office of the Town Council and the former Board School is now the Arthur Mee centre, part of Broxtowe College, Chilwell. This commemorates one of the town's famous sons, Arthur Mee, a journalist and author who founded the *Childrens' Newspaper* and the King's England series of county books. There are

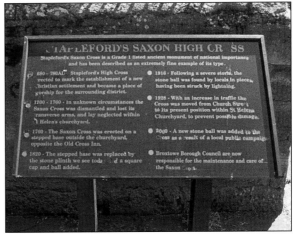

Stapleford's most historic structure, the Saxon Cross in St Helen's churchyard, has this information board alongside it.

still some reminders of the past. The Saxon Cross has survived for 1,000 years despite being moved around and as the most important Saxon work in the county must be protected for all time. Wesley's Chapel and the weavers' houses nearby on Nottingham Road are reminders of the 18th century.

Stapleford at the dawn of the 20th century by Barbara Brooke and Nigel Brooks has been published since the Thoroton Society *Bibliography* was written, and Stapleford District and Local History Society have produced a Town Trail.

The remains of an earlier bridge over the railway near the former station can be seen from the newer bridge.

WEST BRIDGFORD

The name of this suburb means exactly what it says – a place with a bridge near a ford. The bridge in this case was not the sort of structure we now associate with the name. The bridge in question had been built by AD920, as it is recorded as an entry in the *Anglo-Saxon Chronicle*. A bridge in early times was a name given to a crossing of a river at a shallow point, which may have been a kind of pavement.

In the Domesday Book the village or manor of Bridgford was spelled Brigeforde, and William Peverel had jurisdiction with half a plough in lordship and there were three freemen, four villagers and two small-holders with 42 ploughs and 12 acres of meadow. This was much smaller than the other village a few miles downstream, also spelled Brigeforde, where there were 38 men as well as a church and priest. Eventually to prevent confusion the latter was called East Bridgford to distinguish it from West Bridgford.

Dr Thoroton included the adjoining manors of Gamston and Adbolton in his chapter on West Bridgford, but the latter was in the parish of Holme Pierrepont, while there always seems to have been some doubt about whether Gamston was partly in

The Poplars on Rectory Road was built in the 1800s for the Hornbuckle family. It survived for 150 years when it was demolished and a block of flats with the same name built on the site.

Bridgford or not. Thoroton traced the lordship of the manor from the reign of Richard I in the 12th century. Geoffrey Lutterel died in 1417 without children and the land went to Godfrey Hilton, who had married Lutterel's sister. Another Godfrey died aged 15 in 1472 and the land passed to his sister Elizabeth's husband Richard Thimelby. In 1598 Sir Henry Pierrepont became the owner of the estate, which passed eventually to his grandson the Marquis of Dorchester. The estate was then

This was one of the last surviving cottages in the heart of the old village, situated on what became Gordon Road.

Nottingham Forest's football ground and the boathouses were still in the city when this photograph was taken from Trent Bridge. The boundary was adjusted to put them into West Bridgford in 1952.

purchased by Sir John Musters who in Thoroton's time had also acquired the Colwick estate from Sir James Stonehouse. John Throsby, in his addition to Thoroton's account, said that there had been a story that Sir John Musters had acquired the land from the Byron family by winning at cards. As Throsby pointed out, Thoroton's account proved that the report was wrong. One hundred years later, a similar report appeared in newspapers stating that Mrs Musters had acquired the West Bridgford land by winning at cards from the Marquis of Dorchester, which is equally erroneous.

West Bridgford had no church recorded in the Domesday Book, but St Giles, the present church, has its original west tower from early mediaeval times. Its parish registers commenced in 1559 and for 1593 record that plague was prevalent and that Walter Langton and his wife had both died from it and were buried on the same day. Ten burials took place between 17 December and 12 January 1594.

The Protestation Return of 1641/2 contained 97 names, including men from Bassingfield and Gamston. Although the instructions were that men over 18 were to be asked to sign, West Bridgford's list included those over 16 years old. As in 23 instances the surnames occurred twice or more, the list indicates that there were probably only about 60 separate families. The Hearth Tax return for 1674 contains 37 names of those who paid tax but there is no record of houses which were not chargeable. Mrs Greathead, widow of a former

rector, had a house, no doubt the rectory, with eight hearths, but most of the others had only one or two.

In 1685 West Bridgford was the scene of a remarkable robbery. This was carried out on a carriage on Loughborough Road by Edward Brady and Joan Phillips, a Northamptonshire farmer's daughter. Joan, aged 29, was described as having a fine form, with a face of more than ordinary beauty but artful and daring. The pair had carried out a number of similar crimes but on this occasion they were captured. Brady was killed trying to escape but Joan Phillips, who was dressed as a man, was tried at the Assizes and found guilty. She was hanged on a gallows on Wilford Lane near the spot where the hold-up took place.

Not far from this spot there was, until the late 19th century, a pond and a stone effigy of what appears to be a mediaeval knight. This is now in St Giles's Church and is known as the Stone Man.

The village was purely agricultural and its former open fields had been enclosed before Thoroton's time. Its soil in the Trent valley would be good alluvial deposits for arable farming with higher ground to the south for pastures. The inhabitants in 1485 would no doubt have witnessed the troops of King Richard III marching southwards from the meadows below Nottingham Castle to Bosworth Field where the victorious Henry Tudor became Henry VII. Probably the next exciting event would have been in the Civil War when skirmishes between Royalist troops from Newark and the Parliamentarians from Nottingham took place around Trent Bridge.

The 18th century saw two improvements in transport in England to assist the growth of trade. Turnpike roads with tolls meant better maintenance of them, while canals provided cheaper transport of heavy loads. Both these took place in West Bridgford but only on the fringes of the parish. Turnpike roads were established between 1737 and 1759 on what are now Radcliffe, Loughborough and Melton Roads. The 1796 Grantham canal fell into the Trent near Lady Bay and separated the part of West Bridgford east of the canal from the rest.

The lords of the manor, the Musters, did not live in West Bridgford since they had Colwick Hall, but in 1768 Mundy Musters started to build the red-brick Hall which is still a focal point of the old village. It was completed in 1774 but apart from John Musters's married daughter none of the family ever lived there. The rector's widow lived there for a time and then in around 1838 it was let to Lewis Heymann. He was a German lace merchant who visited England in the course of his trade and when he married he decided to settle in England, becoming a naturalised citizen. He carried on a lace curtain manufacturing business known as Heymann and Alexander. He was elected as an alderman on the Nottingham Town Council and was mayor in 1857. He was a prominent member of the High Pavement Unitarian Chapel in Nottingham. He died in 1869 leaving an estate valued at £250,000.

At the first census of 1801 the population of West Bridgford was 235 and by 1881 it was still only 293. As West Bridgford adjoined the Meadows district of the borough, which was an industrial suburb in 1881, it is surprising that West Bridgford was still a small agricultural village. This must have been a deliberate policy of John Chaworth-Musters, who had married a wealthy heiress, Mary Chaworth. That the estate was prosperous is shown

One of the open-top buses of the Urban District Council's transport undertaking, which started in 1913 and was taken over by Nottingham City Transport in 1968. (LSL)

by records of the administration of it in the period from 1810 to 1830, which have survived. John Musters was still living at Colwick Hall, but he also had a town house in London, as his wife was a lady-in-waiting to the Queen. The management of the two estates, Colwick and West Bridgford, was carried out by a Nottingham solicitor's partnership, Jamson and Leeson, who collected the rents and kept the accounts. These reveal that in 1811 the rental income from West Bridgford was £2,004 a year, Colwick £2,014 and Sneinton £220, a total of £4,238 a year.

There was a tithe award drawn up in 1838, which was accompanied by a map with references to each holding as set out in the award. This gave the occupier's name, names of fields, whether arable or pasture and the acreage. The parish was mainly owned by the Musters family, apart from 60 acres owned by Clifford Caunt. He had inherited this from a Miss Hornbuckle, the last surviving member of a family mentioned as early as the 16th century.

The 1881 census of 293 people was the last one of the village, as is evidenced by the figures of 2,502 in 1891 and 7,018 in 1901, which showed it to have become a town. Most of the new dwellings built to house the increased population were in what was then known as New Bridgford. It was concentrated in the north of the district, along

Radcliffe Road, Bridgford Road, Musters Road and Loughborough Road.

The new creation was a planned one. Whether John Chaworth-Musters's decision to sell off land for building plots was due to falling farm rents or because of increasing urban land values is not known. A regular street plan from Trent Bridge southwards set out the areas to be developed, with some of the street names being from names of the Chaworth-Musters family. Covenants as to the minimum size and values of the larger houses on the main road were also specified, along with prohibitions against use for trades.

The lordship of the manor was sold to a London merchant, Alderman Sir Horatio Davies, together with large areas of land. Albert Heymann, the son of Lewis Heymann, had continued to live at the Hall, which he purchased.

This new estate attracted many businessmen from Nottingham, including lace and hosiery manufacturers, owners of retail shops and professional men. Some smaller houses were built to rent to less affluent people, but these were mainly better-paid working men such as foremen, clerks and warehousemen. The early arrivals soon formed a Local Board of Health, which from 1895 became an Urban District Council. The council continued

When open-top buses travelled along Bridgford Road and drew near to the railway bridge, the conductors warned the passengers not to stand up under the bridge. (LSL)

to uphold the character of the area as envisaged by the former owner. A number of different nonconformist churches were built and there was a Defence Association. This was not to repel invaders from Nottingham, but to oppose any applications for public house licences. It was able to do so successfully until 1936. The town continued to expand until 1914 but resumed growth from 1920, this time with more modern, mainly smaller houses, mostly south of Melton Road. This growth was assisted by the council starting its own omnibus undertaking in 1913, although this faced difficulties during the war. A feature of this period was the increase in the number of commercial travellers, so much so that the council held its elections on Mondays, before the travellers left on business.

A notable event in 1923 was the purchase by the Urban District Council of the Hall and its grounds. The Hall became the council's offices and the grounds were laid out as a park. A less welcome event was the action of the city in attempting to bring West Bridgford and other adjacent areas within its boundaries. This was fiercely opposed by the Urban District Council, as was a similar attempt in 1931, both successfully. In 1935 the urban district was extended to include Edwalton and Wilford, although this had little effect until after World War Two.

New schools and shops had been built from the 1890s onwards, and further development of this nature took place alongside residential building at Wilford Hill and Edwalton, as well as in the older parts, which saw the final disappearance of farms and cottages. In 1952, an adjustment of the boundary with Nottingham City brought to an end a somewhat anomalous situation whereby part of Bridgford lay north of the River Trent, while a much larger part of Nottingham was south of the river. The centre of the river bed became the boundary, which meant Bridgford had half of Trent Bridge, while County Hall, started in 1936, and Nottingham Forest football ground also became

One of West Bridgford's amateur sport teams, football if the boots are a clue, about to depart for an away match. (LSL)

part of West Bridgford and the area of Nottinghamshire County Council.

In 1974 the Urban District Council ceased and West Bridgford became part of Rushcliffe Borough Council, which has its headquarters in the former Bridgford Hotel. The latter part of the 20th

This large farmhouse was at the corner of Bridgford Road and Rectory Road and was demolished in the 1960s. The site was used for new premises for what is now British Telecom. (LSL)

century was a period of many changes in West Bridgford. Road traffic, particularly in the mornings and evenings has become much heavier with the growth of commuter villages in the south of the county. This has been alleviated, in part, by road alterations around Trent Bridge, and by the construction of a new stretch of the A52 road to by-pass the town. The closing of the railway, with the demolition of three of its bridges, allowed a new road bridge at Lady Bay to be made on the old railway track.

Further residential development on the west side, at Wilford Hill in the 1950s, has been followed by a new suburb, Compton Acres. The part of Wilford beyond the former LNER line had been transferred to the city in 1952. A similar development on the east side has been at Gamston, which although adjoining both West Bridgford and Edwalton may not consider itself part of Bridgford.

Central Avenue in the 1950s before the Tudor Cinema, partly visible on the left, was demolished. (LSL)

Industry has never been able to gain a foothold in West Bridgford, which remains residential with modern leisure facilities, care homes, a health centre, a large hypermarket and services such as banks and building societies as well as a Test Match standard cricket ground which television commentators refer to as being in Nottingham.

Published in 2001, *West Bridgford Past* is the first comprehensive history of the village-to-town since 1914.

Index